Published by Little Toller Books in 2021

Text © Simon Moreton 2021

The right of Simon Moreton to be identified as the author of this work has been asserted by him in accordance with Copyright, Design and Patents Act 1988

Illustrations, jacket artwork and design © Simon Moreton 2021

Typeset in Garamond by Little Toller Books

We have made every effort to trace the copyright-holders; in the event of any inadvertent omission or error please notify Little Toller Books.

Printed in UK by TJ Books

All papers used by Little Toller Books are natural, recyclable products made from wood grown in sustainable, well-managed forests

A catalogue record for this book is available from the British Library

ISBN 978-1-908213-87-7

WHERE?

Simon Moreton

LITTLE TOLLER BOOKS

27.4.94   Simon Moreton   **Exploring Attitudes and Values**

All about me

Please complete the following unfinished sentences with an immediate response ... a 'gut' reaction.

I like ...... Art, Mark, my family, various friends, guitar various foods, cats, Sci.Fi. Nature

I hate big Dogs, Justin S█████████

I am happy when ...... Things go right for me, my dad comes home

I am unhappy when ...... my pets die, moving house. I hear here about endangered species.

I get angry when ...... people abuse animals, My brother annoys me, when I get blamed for things I didn't do.

The most important thing in life for me is ...... Art, cats and my family.

The best measure of personal success is ...... Learning that I could draw

What I admire most in other people is ...... modesty, kindness.

What I dislike most in other people is ...... selfishness, immodesty.

The epitaph I would like most is ...... "A kind boy who enjoyed life and loved cats"

If I could have one wish it would be ...... to never die.

'Down in yonder meadow there is a little house, and in that little house there is a little room, and in that little room there is a little shelf, and on that little shelf there is a little cup, and in that little cup there is something I would not take all the world for.'

Traditional Shropshire riddle

Loveliest of trees, the cherry now
Is hung with bloom along the bough,
And stands about the woodland ride
Wearing white for Eastertide.

A. E. Housman, *A Shropshire Lad*

Preface

When my Dad turned sixty, I promised him a painting.

One reason I made this promise was because the summer after finishing university I had moved home and agreed to keep my unemployed self useful by painting my parents a painting for their newly decorated sitting room. I was not – and am not – a gifted painter, and the painting in question is categorically Not A Good Painting. Nonetheless, it has hung – been hanged – on one wall or another wherever my parents have lived for the past fifteen years. I find it somewhat mortifying, but Dad had said he'd only take it down if I made him something with which to replace it. So the first reason for offering a new painting was a selfish one.

The second reason was because the painting I wanted to replace, and the painting I wanted to replace it with, were supposed to depict somewhere that was very important to our family and I thought Dad – having at the point of his sixtieth birthday recently retired – might like to have a more thoughtful memento of that place than the odd, dull, grey-beige *thing* that I had previously given him. So the second reason was probably (a little bit) less selfish.

The painting was going to be of Titterstone Clee Hill in Shropshire, where Dad had worked as an engineer on a radar station. Shropshire, most maps will tell you, sits in the West Midlands, on the border between England and Wales. Cheshire lies to the north, Staffordshire to the east, and Herefordshire and Worcestershire to the south. Wales is due west.

We lived in the borderlands, halfway between the larger towns of Shrewsbury to the north and Leominster to the south, in a little village called Caynham. It was all very picturesque, and a time our family remembers fondly.

In 2017, Dad got ill and died. Cancer and premature death are a fucker for playing with the things you once imagined static or stable, so it's no surprise that during the period of his illness thoughts about growing up, of how our family came to be and where we were from bubbled up as we sought in trauma and in grief to find common narratives to our diverging life-courses, things that would keep us connected with him and each other.

With all this in mind, the idea of a painting started to feel insufficient, and wanting to know more about where I had grown up and whether knowing more would make any difference to me, the painting became this book.

So, this book is (mostly) about that one specific place where my Dad worked, and that one specific place where my family lived; it is being written in lieu of that painting, like one big apology for ever having started this whole 'painting' business in the first place. I hope this settles the debt, though I no longer know what that debt is, or to whom it is owed.

S. M.
Bristol, 2021

Mum

We are in a calm ward with machines beeping and loads of questions being asked behind closed curtains. Safe journey

Still being triaged no sign of consultants though. No idea

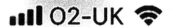 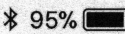

Si dad's breathing has changed

We're in the car 15 mins away

Ok

2 Mar 2017, 11:17

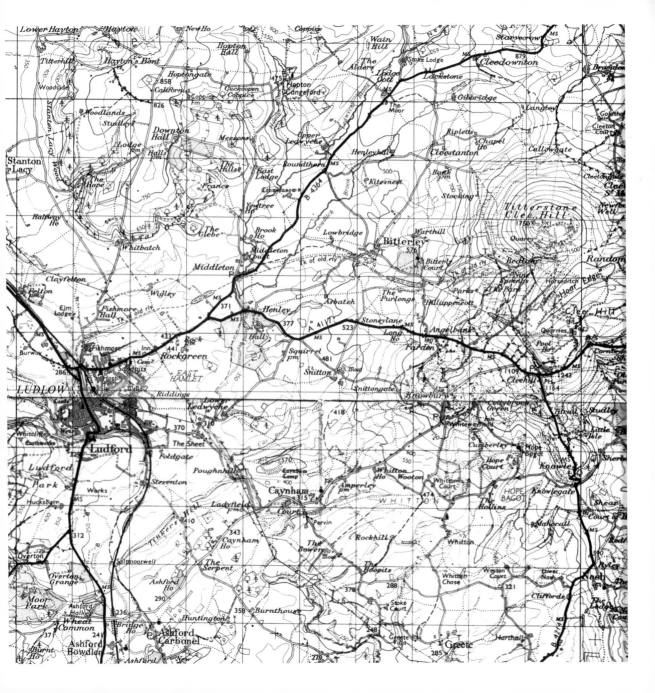

TITTERSTONE.

The lane is narrow and crooked which leads from here to Clee Stanton, where there are one or two farms at the foot of the mountain, at which a vehicle can be put up while the hill is explored. Very few fields then intervene, and the open hillside is soon reached, covered with bracken and crowned with crags, like its bigger brothers in Wales ; for the basaltic rocks at this end, unlike the more southern portion, are untouched, except by the action of the elements, and the splintered and shapeless masses that have toppled from the upper ledges lie in a slope of wreckage, which is far from easy to climb. On the apex itself a group of huge blocks is traditionally known as the Giant's Chair ; the whole scene being weird and savage to a degree suggestive of the goblins and malignant spirits which were supposed to haunt this spot, which the foxes have now to themselves. It is said that a rocking stone once existed here, and that from it the name of Titterstone is derived. There is a bank surrounding the space on the summit, and a number of smaller circles within, all having the appearance of artificial enclosures, though not sufficiently well preserved to be explainable. Coal was got here with other minerals in the time of Leland, but in recent times the supply has run short, except on the north-east and south slopes, and at Knowbury, where the pits are still worked.

Prologue

February 2016. Ali and I are paying a visit to Titterstone Clee on our way back to Bristol from Manchester, where we have just attended her grandad's funeral. We already had a long weekend booked in Shropshire, and in the end the service coincided with our holiday.

The funeral, two days before Ali's birthday, has somewhat taken the sheen off our visit. We drive up the hill in my dented Honda Civic that belonged first to Dad, then to my brother, Tim. When he emigrated to a mysterious tech job in the States, he gave it to me, complete with a boot full of half-empty booze bottles, a yucca, a coffee machine, half an ice-cream-maker, and a twig in a pot.

'Look after the pomegranate,' he texted me later, 'it's special to us.' I promised I would, but in truth the twig had never left the Oxfordshire car park from which I had picked up the car a week after he had arrived in California; I thought it was dead, so I had ditched it.

At that point, the car itself was only five years old and far more space-age than the much-loved sit-on-mower of a car that I had owned before and had called the Beast, precisely because it wasn't one. Our step-grandfather Roy had owned a Honda Civic too, and Tim and I remember him taking us on increasingly perilous trips around the south coast in the summer weeks that we'd spend with him and our Nan – my mum's mum – near misses and racist slurs demurred by Werther's Original and blocky travel sweets. Roy, nonetheless a gentle man, eventually drove his Honda through their garage wall one day, and that was the end of both his car and his driving career.

I wobble the car into the car park. The surface is full of mirrors where rainwater has gathered, the sky on the land, placidly hiding potholes as deep as wells. I stop the car, and we step out gingerly amongst the puddles and schist.

The old quarry face looms. It is cold; snow is on the ground, and the rain is atomising into a hundred thousand tiny blobs. The hill is a tump, a mountain, decorated with quarry scoops and cliffs. Over there, the story goes, they filmed a TV advert telling people not to die of ignorance; over there was a drowned village; over there a cairn; over there radars; over there a burned-out car-scar; out there, beyond the thick wall of cloud, a view so pastoral that Tolkien was alleged to have written about it and called it the Shire.

In 1963, the Civil Aviation Authority opened a radar station in the drystone embankments of an Iron Age hill fort on the top of the hill. My Dad took a job as an engineer there in 1987. He spent many happy days working on this sometimes baking, sometimes frozen, windswept peak, fixing radars, drinking tea and watching birds from the station window.

The radars dotted around the hilltop map the aerospace across the region, feeding data about the whereabouts of planes in the sky to air-traffic controllers all over the country. This was the latest in a wave of innovation on the hill going back thousands of years, from Bronze Age ritual to Iron Age occupation, to coal mining, lime production and stone quarrying, to farming, aviation and meteorology.

'Cle Hills be holy in Shropshire,' wrote John Leland, in his Henry VIII sponsored survey of England, *Itinerary Of John Leland In Or About The Years 1535–1543*. I share this feeling, and it is why I've brought Ali here, to visit the hill and tell her all about my family and our past.

We leave the car park and are suddenly exposed to the north wind and more rain, as the gorse and acid soil and lumps of rock and lumps of sheep wink in and out of focus. We head for the summit.

Dad loved it here. In his day he was one of a team of a dozen or so who ran the site twenty-four hours a day. I never really understood specifically what they did, but he and his colleagues kept the radars working – colleagues like Alan, who would drive to work along the narrow road up to the summit with one hand on the steering wheel, eating his breakfast with the other, and who arrived at the radar station one day, only a little late, but with cornflakes all over the car ceiling, a dented roof and a slightly confused look on his face.

Then there was the other Alan, whose handshake is still very firm, and whose aunt was a potato farmer and primary school teacher who taught us about potato varieties. Once, mistaking me for a troublemaker in the canteen queue, she slapped me across my bare little leg.

'You'd better not be crying, Simon,' she called to me afterwards, in front of the whole school at pickled-beetroot-and-sultana-laced-curry lunch. I was.

There are actually three Clee Hills: Titterstone Clee where my Dad worked, Brown Clee some miles to the north, and a third, somewhat harder to define Clee Hill, an undulation in the same mass of high ground as Titterstone.

'The Highest Parte of Cle Hills is cawlyd Tyderstone,' writes Leland. 'In it is a fayre playne Grene, and a Fountayne in it. There is anothar Hill a 3 miles distaunt from it caulyd The Browne Cle. There is a Chace for Deare. Ther is anothar cawllyd Caderton's Cle, and ther be many Hethe Cokks, and a broket, caulyd Mille Brokcet, springethe in it, and aftar goithe into a Broket cauled Rhe, and Rhe into Tende by neth Tende Bridge.'

Caderton's Cle, by the description, is likely to be what is now Clee Hill, an area of higher land above Cleehill village, to the west of Catherton Common, and due south-southeast of Titterstone's peak. Tende refers to the River Teme; also, Brown Clee (1,770ft) is technically a higher peak than Titterstone Clee (1,749ft).

The views can be spectacular. On August 14, 1855, the Woolhope Club, a group of naturalists, geologists and antiquarians from Hereford, visited Clee. The Honorary Secretary, H. Cecil Moore, wrote all about what they saw on that day:

'a vast range of country ... unsurpassed in natural beauty, presented itself to the admiring eyes of the visitors. The massive Old Red mountains of Radnor Forest, the Hatteral, Scyrrid-fawr and the range of Graig, Garway, Saddlebow and Aconbury; the lofty hills which fringe – if we may so write – the Silurian islet of Woolhope; the noble igneous range of Malvern and Abberley; the broad mass of the Brown Clee, and the picturesque Silurian ridges and peaks of Caer Caradoc and the Stiperstones, successively met the eye as it wandered round the wonderfully beautiful landscape.'

On this trip, however, Brown Clee, with its repeater mast and trees and plane-fuselage-hiding-lake, and even the other Clee, are invisible to us. Instead, we blindly slip and slide up towards the footpath, whose entrance is adjacent to the big gates of the radar station, and which runs along the perimeter fence at the top of an embankment. The weather worsens. I try to speak but the air is blown from my mouth and the words don't even form. I am powerless; I can hardly breathe. After a few more unsteady feet, Ali calls out, shouting, although she's next to me, to say we should probably turn around. She's right; we admit defeat and head back to the car.

Back at the place we're staying – a small cabin built in a Welsh village by a couple for their daughter and her young child – we light a fire to get the rain out of our bones, but the humidity and insulation conspire against us; we are forced to open all the windows and doors to let the accidental sauna cool. The rain steams outside, and the fire goes out.

In the porch, tucked in little pots, are some seedlings – *Erysimum* 'Spice Island', *Erysimum* 'Bowles Mauve', and an unidentified hellebore. Ali's grandad, a keen gardener, had them growing and ready to go for the spring, so we have brought them from Knutsford to plant in our own garden.

Almost one year later will come the phone call, while in Bristol those flowers, now all grown up, will be getting ready to bloom, orange, purple.

One
How it started

The phone call

It was an otherwise unremarkable Tuesday. A meeting had overrun, and I had returned to my desk already in a thoroughly non-committal mood about the day. Outside, the late January sunlight shifted meekly. I could see it through the skylight, which was muddy with moss and seagull footprints. I glanced at my telephone, which I had left on top of a mound of unread papers, some of which bore watermarks acquired from a leak in the windows above.

I noticed I had missed a phone call from my dad. I frowned a little because it wasn't like him to ring me at work. I picked up my phone and hesitantly called him back. It rang a couple of times before he answered.

'Hi Simes,' he said, cheerful enough.

'Hi Dad. You rang? Sorry I missed your call.' I tried to hide the edge in my voice, but I don't think I did a very good job.

'That's OK. How are you? Not too busy?'

Yes, I thought, *why did you ring me?*

'No, no. What's up? Everything OK?'

A nervous grit crept into Dad's voice. 'It's nothing to worry about,' he said. 'I just wanted to ring and let you know... I mean, I thought I should let you know, that, well, maybe this back-ache thing might be something a bit more serious.' Dad had been suffering from back pain since November. A vision of him in Devon at Christmas, doubled-up and largely immobile, paired with Mum's strained cheer, started to return to me. It was a tough December.

'Oh...' I offered, weakly.

Dad continued. 'So you know I finished at the physio before Christmas, and he said I should be fine now, and that I probably just need to build the muscles back up. So I went swimming,' he continued, in a tone that aimed for, but fell short of, carefree. 'I'm a bit out of practice, what with going to see your brother and then the backache when I got back, and Christmas. Anyway, I did a couple of lengths at the pool and I just couldn't catch my breath. It felt like I was just a bit winded. Do you know what I mean?'

By now I had moved to the stairwell. I looked at the empty lift shaft, an architectural anomaly from the redevelopment of the building, an old warehouse. The shaft was never fitted with a lift, so it stands as a hollow four-sided column around which stairs descend to the rear entrance, opposite the Biffa bins and carrot tops and cabbage puddles and chicken smudges that signify a neighbouring restaurant's back door.

Dad spoke again. 'I rang the GP and he booked me an appointment for tomorrow. It's probably nothing, maybe just a chest infection or bronchitis or something, so I'll let you know.'

I breathed in, but couldn't be sure what to say next.

'Like I say, it's nothing to worry about,' he continued. 'I just thought I'd let you know.' He paused. 'It's your Mum I'm worried about. She's convinced it's something a bit more serious. Maybe you could give her a call?'

Fucking hell.

'Of course,' I said.

'Thanks Simes. I'd better go have a cup of tea and ring your brother.'

'Thanks, Dad. Just let me know how it goes with the doctor.'

We said our goodbyes and I ended the call. I sat down at my desk. The front of my brain was burning, almost furious that Dad had called me at work, only to tell me what amounted to not very much.

Slightly dazed, I wandered over to the kitchen area, and on the way glanced through the open boardroom door, out through the big windows that overlooked the harbour. It was still grey. People milled about. An empty houseboat hugged the harbour wall.

Inside the room, chairs and table sat empty.

I recalled a meeting we held in there, one day in November about five years before. We had drifted in listlessly, distracted by one thing or another, and the conversation was slow to start. Through the window I noticed a man walking along the water's edge feeding a taut cord into the black wetness which was carried in front of him by some unseen force, like a dog straining at its leash.

'Looks like a man walking his fish,' I joked.

My colleagues laughed, and we all watched him. A moment or two later, a diver surfaced at the other end of the rope, and slowly the scene thickened in the drizzle: police officers began to appear to calm a gathering crowd. A small boat with a stuttering outboard motor came into view. Another diver surfaced. Then a large form, bulbous with air and water, rose to the surface.

The boat crew and the divers struggled to hoist the shape from the water, by now visible as a mass in a distended body bag. The boat tilted precariously. Someone on the quay broke down, caught by her companion. Someone gasped. Another person turned away. A seagull shat nearby.

The meeting forgotten, we watched the sad transfer, from water, to boat, to stretcher, of the shape. Two men then carried the stretcher up some steps set into the harbour wall, and into a waiting ambulance. The crowd dispersed. We didn't know what to say to one another. No jokes made that moment any less a ghastly voyeuristic act of complicity on our part, guilty and shocked.

Back in the present, such as it was, I poured coffee nervously into a stained mug. Something solid in my head was shifting, like a tectonic plate.

'I thought he was going to tell me he had cancer or something,' I said to my colleague Rosie a few minutes later, trying to make light of the seeping fears percolating through my brain. We made jokes, usual, I imagine, amongst people in their twenties and thirties, about how at some point you just have to let your parents fend for themselves, about becoming their carers, and their moral support in times of hypochondriac crisis.

But I was scared shitless.

Two
Holy Hills

Tyderstone

The Clee hills were born in deep time as one hill beneath a vast, temperate inland sea. Local rumour had it that they were formed from a solitary volcano, but that theory was debunked by enterprising geologists in the 1930s. Instead, it was found to have been lava steaming up through the layers of gradually folding sediment on the sea bed, that together built up what would become the hill; mounds of the earth's belly on top of the plant matter and silt and animals and mud and debris and shit laid down by millennia of weirdo alien sea creatures eating one other, breeding, then dying, on repeat.

After some measure of time far beyond my ability to comprehend, the waters began to recede, exposing the mountain to glaciation, denudation and erosion, which after an even more incomprehensible length of time, split the mountain in two, forming Titterstone and Brown Clees as they stand today.

On Titterstone, subvolcanic intrusions into Old Red Sandstone form its peak, with dolerite flowing down its spine, laid over Cornbrook Sandstone and carboniferous limestone. The igneous capping of all three hills protects the softer rock beneath, preserving coal seams, limestone and other sedimentary deposits.

Titterstone's distinctive profile, like a wave not quite ready to break on a shore, is visible for many miles around. To the east, there is (apparently) no land higher than Clee until you reach Russia, a theoretical sightline unbroken as far as the Urals. One pub on Clee even changed its name to the Kremlin Inn after its jukebox began to mysteriously pick up Russian radio when the weather was just so.

As it happens, the weather is rarely 'just so' on Titterstone. People who live with the hill know this, and are always prepared for its processions of storms and fogs, thick mists, rain and gales, sudden sunshine, eviscerating breezes and awful cold.

Dad had become accustomed to the hill's tantrums, too, and told us all about them. He would describe how the wind would come from nowhere, or he'd get sunburnt on his bald head in a rainstorm, or the temperature would suddenly plummet, and the ground would freeze almost instantly.

Once, he told me over dinner in Devon, he had emerged from an outbuilding only to find the rain had frozen solid in the minutes he was indoors. He was forced to travel back to the safety of the station on his hands and knees, while being buffeted around on the ice rink by the wind, like a feather on a pond.

Snow could be a problem, too. It would come in overnight, blown by the wind into thick and impassable drifts. For those occasions the team at the station owned a Snowcat, a weird caterpillar-tracked vehicle that looked like a cross between a bulldozer and a Lego car, which they kept at a local garage. Dad joked that the special licence he had acquired to drive it meant that he was also allowed to drive tanks.

Storms could be fierce. The *Eddoes Shrewsbury Journal*, from Wednesday July 21, 1880, reports how, 'on Saturday evening last, between sign and nine o'clock, the Clee hill was visited with a dreadful thunderstorm, which lasted about an hour; the vividity of the lightning was magnificently beautiful, the thunder was appalling, and the rain descended in torrents. It is feared that the storm has damaged the gardens and farm crops to a considerable extent.'

We also have a family story about the time Titterstone was hit by a great, wild thunderstorm. Something at the radar station had broken and Dad had been called in to help fix it. For reasons the family forget, he took Tim with him; perhaps Mum and I were out, perhaps it was a school day and Tim was off sick.

At first, it was nothing out of the ordinary – rain, wind, distant thunder. But gradually, the storm worsened. Then the power went out. Glass flexed. The rain thrashed. Tim, Dad and his colleagues were forced to seek refuge in the corridor, away from the big windows. They peered cautiously out through the glass when they dared, only to see lightning begin to strike the tarmac outside, again and again and again, coming closer and closer with each blink.

Then there are the burning hot days when you can see for miles; the sun will be blazing and the clouds will be light like whipped egg whites. In all directions you'll see fields and enclosures, green, brown, pale yellow, the pathways of vivid trees marking the course of rivers and streams, towns and hamlets and villages just visible in the earth's quilty folds.

These are the days people like to remember. We have photos of us running around on the hill in our little shorts, Dad in a hat, Mum enjoying the sun.

But my favourite times are when being on Clee feels like being alone in the heavens. It'll be raining in Ludlow or Caynham or Ashford Boulder or wherever, and from down there the hill's peak will be lost in the murk. But from the summit, above the clouds, the land below goes missing and you find yourself looking onto an eiderdown, almost close enough to reach down and touch, looking for all the world as if you could step off the hill and into its vapours, while a UV-rich blue sky hangs above.

Those times are magical; so magical, in fact, that I don't know if my memories of them are even real.

Three
Diagnosis

Okwell Soov

A week after the phone call, I was sat at Dad's bedside in the Royal Exeter and Devon Hospital. My Mum was elsewhere at another appointment and I was trying very, very hard not to let my thoughts sway to panic as the lung specialist started to speak, softly but deliberately, in a voice with just a hint of a Scottish accent, about scans and blood tests and x-rays and infections and pleural effusions and tumours and who knows what else.

Have you experienced this? Been the one in the bed, the one in the chair next to the bed, the one breaking the news? Being part of that little trinity, I naively thought, was something that happened to other people and it's a truism, but yes, I am other people to you and you are to me. So there we go.

After Dad was discharged, blood drawn, scans made, results pending, I helped him, wheezing and in pain, to my car and drove him and Mum back to their house on the Devon coast, all three of us in a different kind of agony.

Three days after the first visit to hospital we were back in Bristol when Dad called me. He told me through both our tears that the diagnosis was lung cancer which had already spread to his liver, to his bones and who knows where else.

I told him I loved him, and he told me he loved me too. I hung up and in a daze I wandered into the spare room at the top of the stairs. Ali joined me as I looked out of the window. The raindrops colonising the outside of the glass began to roll down in little lines and I was reminded of watching rain streak along the outside of windows from the back seat of the family car. I didn't know what do.

The next day, Ali and I both called in sick to work and we spent a few days listlessly walking around Bristol in shock. Her father had been diagnosed with bowel cancer in November. We had barely known how to handle that, so this news just compounded a terrible sense of dread.

I spoke to my parents every day. Mum was worried; Dad's condition seemed to be worsening. My parents seemed paralysed by the news, a claustrophobic inertia crawling into their voices at the other end of the telephone. None of us seemed to know what was happening nor what to do about it. Things seemed inevitable: Dad wouldn't fuss, and Mum was scared that the worst was already happening.

'Take him to hospital,' I pleaded, my voice aching like a bruised rib.

'He has an appointment on Friday.'

'Ring them, take him sooner.'

She did, and on a cold Friday I drove to Devon to visit him in hospital for a second time, seven days since my previous visit; Yeo Ward, first bed on the right, by the window.

Doctors told us that the pain he was experiencing was due to the calcium building up in his blood, released from his dissolving bones. It was a side effect of the cancer, but not the cancer, and was something treatable.

Your mind does strange things at times like this and I quietly started to wonder about miraculous cures or old wisdom, anything to bring hope. On Titterstone Clee, they used to make a poultice called okwell soov. It was a cure-all cream for cuts, bruises, sickness and pretty much anything that caused you trouble.

There were other remedies from Shropshire, too. If you had a stubborn splinter – like that time I fell into a hawthorn hedge on my friends' farm and I had a thorn stuck in my palm for a week – you could draw it out by tracing a circle with your middle finger around and around the briar, or by making the sign of the cross above it, or laying a fox's tongue over the wound so it could suck out the wood. If you cut yourself with a knife, it was said, you should immediately stick the blade responsible into a side of bacon, which would prevent the wound from festering, then you should read from the Scriptures to stem the flow of blood. To cure a toothache, carry a cadaver's front tooth or apply a mustard plaster to the wrist. An addled goose egg is good for an adder's bite. Tricklings, sheep's dung, could cure smallpox, while grease from the Oswestry church bells clears ringworm. Iron coffin nails could be worn as a charm against rheumatism, and you can drink saffron water to cure jaundice.

To save your lungs from consumption, get up before sunrise, cut a turf from the ground, and, every day for nine mornings lift the sod and breathe into the soil. For whooping cough, put the head of a frog in your mouth, pluck a hair from the cross of a donkey, or go round and round the piebald horse nine times or pass the afflicted child nine times under and over a bramble which has rooted at both ends in an arch across a parish boundary, or take the child to Ludlow Castle and let it call into the old corners, 'Echo, please take away my cough!'

Dad responded well to the conventional treatments. He perked up over the weekend and became almost cheerful. Over the next few days he underwent radiotherapy on his pelvis to target the rot, and on his eye where free-floating cancer molecules had left his osseous tissues behind and lodged in his iris. Common, apparently, but who knew?

Despite being in a perpetual present of scans and tests, drugs and hospital noises, Dad joked with the nurses, and talked to his ward mates. His optimism, his faith in science was almost too much to behold.

His manner also changed. He became a bit fuzzy, a bit bristly, a little manic; I don't think any of us was prepared for him to be not quite himself, but it made sense – with the steroids, the morphine and all the other stuff he was being given. Why don't they tell you this?

We stayed at my parents' house and muddled through as best we could. We visited him most days. We tried not to worry too much about anything other than the present.

I doubt there's still a person alive who knows how to make okwell soov.

Four
Where we lived

PLAN OF THE PARISH OF

CAINHAM IN

THE

County of Salop

LUDFORD PARISH

Cainham Camp

LUDFORD PARISH

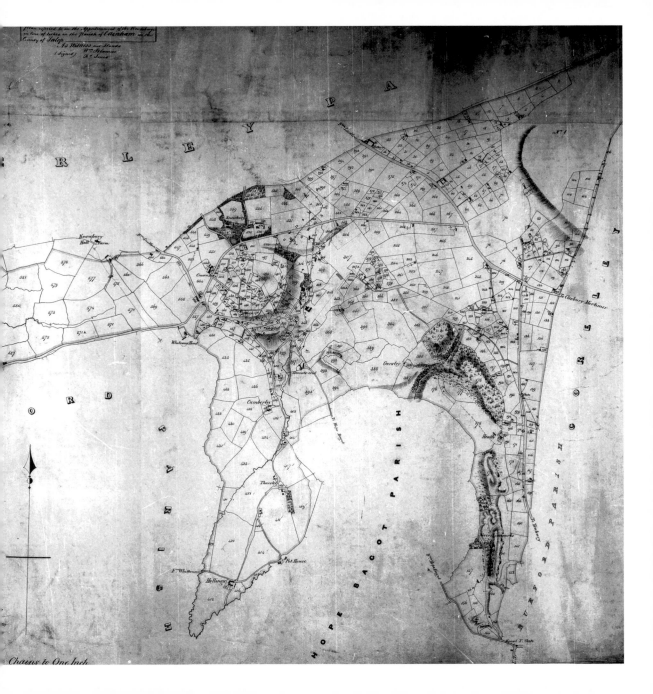

Timothy Moreton

Introduction

My house is positioned in the country, in the Caynham Court estate. It was built facing north-east, looking towards Titterstone Clee. It was completed in May 87 and we moved in September of the same year. Therefore we were the first people living there.
It is a detached house, with 2 quite large gardens, one at the front and one at the back. It is quite a tall house.

A Build up of My house

Firstly, it is a square shaped house, about 9 by 9 metres.....

...Next we have a small, half hexagon which is placed in the centre of the front face of our cube.....

...On the front, to the left of the hexagon are two windows (see Appendix) on top of each other.....

...And the same for the other side...

....Now we have the front door. It is positioned at the bottom of the front face of the hexagon and coloured brown, with a brass handle and letter-box, with a large number `5` at the top....

....And the bathroom window above it....

Door

..Down the other side of the house is a gate.....And a short brick
wall running along the the side of the house....

...And two sets of steps cutting it short....Along with the fence
panel by the gate, the path along the wall and up the steps to the
front door and the fence panels the other side.

Now the large front garden. The silver birch in the middle of the
garden.....the low fence running between us and our neighbours
gardens. The other windows round the side of the house with the
gate...And the door by the far, bottom window...And you mustn`t
forget the garage...positioned on the side of the house with gate...
It has a double car capacity and we use it for storing all our junk
in.

Caynham

Caynham sits about three miles down the hill from Titterstone Clee. Although the parish of the same name is a widely distributed series of farms and hamlets and small housing estates across Clee and its southwestern slopes, the village itself is tiny. It is strung along the lower reaches of the road to the hill, clustering around a church (twelfth century), a village hall (twentieth century) and a now-closed school (nineteenth century), all under the watchful promontory of Caynham Camp, a hill fort (*c.* eighth century BC).

We lived in a newly built house at the bottom of a little incline, tucked off the main road between Ludlow and Clee. Ours was one of a couple of dozen houses built around the diminishing activities of a commercial turkey farm and the remnants of an empty stately home, Caynham Court. We lived next door to the remains of its walled gardens which were full of rubble and dock. We called it 'the dump'.

I went to school first in nearby Ludlow – Sandpits, Clee View, got bullied; tough class, tough kids, tough lives, forgotten families out in the fields and the estates – before changing school to the village school, country kids, a different pace, sheep in the school field.

In the general vicinity of where we lived there were a lot of woods, fields and farms. It was very quiet – quieter than suburban Surrey where we'd lived before (darker, too – no streetlights), except when the birds sang and the sun came up and it was as loud and bright as any town.

Next to the Court there was an old saggy caravan that sat like a chest with its ribs showing. I can still see it clearly. My brother struggles to recall this, but once we tried to use Blu Tack as an explosive in the caravan's padlock, because it looked like something we'd seen on TV, but of course we didn't have any matches and Blu Tack isn't an explosive.

We did eventually get inside when the fibreglass and plywood gave in like wet cardboard and the door buckled, revealing a damp, rotten lung. I don't remember what was inside: papers, a coffee cup overflowing with mould, mud, gold, a murder victim, or maybe nothing.

Caynham Court itself sat abandoned and boarded up behind our house. It grew out of the rubble and grass and brambles like a brick plant. It had past lives – a Jacobean manor house, come and gone; an eighteenth-century stately home; a wartime evacuation for the Lancing College private school, boys living and being taught while the war came across the sea; later, Hillhampton House for girls, Miss Liesching teaching home economics and household skills; then, later still, offices for a turkey hatchery, then vacant.

It was a concrete time machine. You could smell its spores and dampness and cold, undisturbed air through cracks in the brickwork. There were glimpses to be had of the interior; there was a toilet block with its rear wall demolished, exposing the porcelain to the elements, but with the door connecting to the main building sealed off; from the locked patio doors, glass still intact, you could see directly through a drawing room, to a bookshelf which miraculously still heaved with books.

Caynham Court at its peak presided over five hundred acres of parkland and walled gardens, mounted on a haha tipping away to the Ledwyche Brook which flowed south past the estate. There were also kennels, farmland, stables and a mill. *The County Seats Of Shropshire: A Series Of Descriptive Sketches, With Historical And Antiquarian Notes, Of The Principal Family Mansions* contains a pencil sketch of the Court, looking out west from the tree-line of the neighbouring woodland, across a landscaped moat. The curdled remains of the crossing point, a decorative iron bridge, were still present when Tim and I would sneak into those woods. The bridge looked like a tangled, rusty climbing frame. We'd slide down the ditch bank, through our neighbours' grass clippings and bin bags. Then we'd explore. First the flowing water of the Ledwyche, then the plantations of trees, incongruous bamboos amongst birches and flowering nettles. Then, with our backs to the brook, and facing up the hill, we'd seek out the redwood, whose crown you could see from our house, and touch its papery, coconut-husk bark. We built dens. My cousin Ewan did a poo behind a bush up there.

Here, life crawled like a dream. I'd lie in bed in the mornings, awake at sunrise, long grey curtains over sash windows. Sometimes I'd creep across my room to wave at the bin men, and they'd wave back. In the cold grey paper dawn I'd listen to the wood pigeons. I knew, very particularly, that they were doctors of some sort. I didn't know their motives, but I was convinced they were up to something sinister, hoo-hoo-hooing across the dump from the woods.

A slate roof amplified the rain noise. The Great Storm of 1987 took a tile and threw it, corner down, into the front lawn so it looked like a standing stone. One autumn the leatherjackets came out like a mini-plague, undulating through the grass and across the paving slabs of the garden path, while in the summer, life on the patio was red mites the colour of a word processor spelling error.

In the back garden the earth was wet, there was the smell of grass, in the spring morning, in the winter wind, in the March frost or under the brown humus sluice of autumn. We climbed the walnut tree that grew there, our own little river flowing from the sky. There were streams of white bark, and small, black knots tarred shut, like rocks in the rapids. The leaves were its banks, full in June, spare in December. We canoed up and down, learning the nooks and pools of each crook, and the best places to sit and dangle our feet. I never got stuck, and I never fell out.

We'd play on the back lawn in the summer until a storm turned silent jaundiced skies into black clouds and the tension would yield and we'd run around, picking up our toys in a bid to get inside, darting between the giant raindrops before there were no gaps of dry air left to occupy; in the garage, Dad taught us to make things out of wood, and cooked whitebait on a camping stove.

It was living here that I fell in love with the natural world. Everything was connected, wild, confusing, terrifying and comforting. I didn't think of what people did as being separate from what the birds and the beasts did. Homes popped out of the ground like shrubs. People planted fences in the same way that the maroon docks seeded themselves in piles of builders' waste. The earth birthed blue and white crockery pieces, while berries grew on barbed wire, and television aerials throbbed with incoming cartoon energy. I came to know – without even realising it – the smell of thousands of years of stratifying, rolling earth, of sheep wool and cow shit and clay soil and rotting leaves, and the bright voltage of water.

I watched the purple plummish damsons ripen in the hedge opposite our house, plump like wrens. They hung by a gap in the foliage that dropped to a wonky plank of wood, pitched over a squelch of a ditch. I'd walk to the village school over that improvised bridge, up the small bank on the other side, over the fence and into the school field.

I read fantasy paperbacks containing things I understood and things I didn't, but which I loved unconditionally – swords and landscapes, all of that, and the cover art – oh my, the covers!

I learned about the vegetable patch with its potatoes, clay pipes and slug traps full of home-brewed beer; about the mysteries of the garage, with its tea chests and garden toys, Dad's white cupboard with boxes of capacitors and screws; about the green oil tank behind the little bit of fence, with the plunge button you'd press to see how much oil was available; and about how the hornbeam Dad planted grew, and why he'd have his photo taken next to it every year.

I danced around to 'Smooth Criminal' in my bedroom, but didn't understand that Michael Jackson had multi-tracked his voice on his recordings (it took me years – and I mean years – to work that out). I just thought all of his backing singers sounded exactly like him.

I learned to swim but wouldn't put my head under the water. I learned what a horse sounded like when it farted, and how not to be scared of cows.

Before I moved to the village school, I was a quiet child. While other children – alluring, unpredictable and unknowable – paired off like swans, roamed in packs, floated around like seeds on the wind, or fought like dust storms, I worked through various fixations: with birds and trees, with Michael Jackson, the animal kingdom, dinosaurs, astronomy, orcs, goblins, wizards and hobbits. I was bemused by my classmates at school in Ludlow who accused me of reading the encyclopaedia for fun as if that was a bad thing. Of course I did. Who wouldn't?

I stuck my face in books about magic and about animals and animal tracks and I didn't know about sport as practice, nor sport as a culture; I tended to catch balls designed for my hands with my face, and balls designed for my feet with my hands. I remember how heavy the football was when I tried to kick it in my oversized studded boots during PE lessons in the muddy field. I was small for my age and my ankles were pampas.

I didn't know the language of bodies and clothes and names and numbers and stadium locations. I was more interested in the walnuts from the tree, marvelling at the black stains of their desiccating skins, monitoring them as they dried on the rack propped up by bricks at the side of the house, or watching them pickle in jars at the back of the cupboard, like little woody cortexes bobbing around in ink.

I did not know 'teams' and when I started at the village school, all the boys liked Liverpool FC. 'Who do you support?' they asked on my first day. I didn't even understand the question, so there wasn't any time to make up a lie. I had never grown up thinking that not knowing about football or rugby or racing or horses or cricket was a bad thing. Thankfully, neither did these boys. They weren't like the other boys I had met by that point in my life; they just shrugged and tried to teach me to play football.

I sometimes think it would be nice to go back and feel like that again, and sometimes I am glad I never can.

Monday 2nd April   Simon Moreton

Sadness

what makes me sad is when some on
if I feel lonely when a membe of
the family dies. Or if someone's ill. Or I se
a dead animals one of my friends that wasgoin
to wales they saw a fox in the middle of th
Road it jumped one the bonnet and got
his head stuck in the wind screen wipers
that's what made me sad.

Five
When I'm sixty-four

Will you still need me?

Not long after dad was diagnosed, we were sat in the car in the driveway preparing to drive to the hospital. I was fiddling with the radio from the passenger seat. Mum was behind the wheel getting ready to start the car. Ali was in the back seat.

The Beatles song 'When I'm Sixty-four' came on the radio, crackly and quiet.

'Will you still need me...'

At this point, Dad was sixty-three.

When I was younger, life beyond thirty didn't exist. I believed at fourteen, fifteen, sixteen that I was done by thirty; mortgaged and dull, with no cultural agency, no relevance, no chance to do anything important. Break the mould now, I thought, or be forever moulded.

I remember once, when I was about eighteen years old, I was sat in my best friend's parked car, talking angrily about how hopeless everything was for me. I was back from university for Easter break, full of my own woes and terrified of ending up as a boring grown-up; a relationship had sputtered out; university wasn't what I expected; I don't know. The sadness and anger were genuine, but my fear was filtered through privilege without the experience to know any better.

So there I was, ranting away in the evening air, windows open slightly, smoking aggressively, waving despondent ash around Bunty the Toyota Corolla, and my friend just suddenly lost it. What happened next, we remember in different ways, but I'm fairly sure he shouted at me – very reasonable under the circumstances – conveying to me that perhaps I was being more than a little self-centred, and that perhaps I might like to consider how lucky I was; I had left home, whilst further education had kept him living at his parents' house.

He was working in a pub, serving the 'regulars' and 'fun guy' lonely alcoholics, being determined not to become one, while at the same time, finding himself left behind in the wake of the progress being made in his friends' lives. Did I realise how myopic I was being, and that actually, life for us was Pretty OK, so why not stop whining and start living? He stopped shouting, seethed for a bit, and then very suddenly started the car, driving off roughly and loudly into the suburban night, shocking me into silence.

Despite my friend's prescient intervention, these feelings persisted throughout my twenties. I spent that decade in a strange bubble of atemporality – not letting myself have a future, resisting the conversation, refusing to take part; not because I was out there living in the 'here and now' or anything righteous or radical. Quite the opposite. I just didn't know what the fuck to do or how to do it. Do any of us?

I don't think my Dad ever quite had the luxury of this way of thinking. I know that he shared some of these feelings – about conforming and not being particularly bothered about being like other people. But he also didn't take those thoughts so seriously that he could indulge them – or maybe his circumstances didn't allow him to; he just sort of got on with things.

My dad Worked. He always Worked. From a teenager loading and unloading lorries at the haulage firm that his Dad worked for in Maidstone, to his apprenticeship at the Civil Aviation Authority and his forty-year career with them, he always worked hard. For us, for himself, for fun, for other people. He had his crises of faith, his fair share of disillusionment and professional disappointments, strained times and hard choices. But he always appeared – at least to me – to have faced them down.

His fears about getting older were different to mine. Whilst I had developed a middle-class, post-end-of-history fear of a blank, meaningless future (and had – arguably – inherited the opportunities to avoid one), Dad's fear was one born of his upbringing; he was worried about the inevitability of illness, and perceived his genetic, working-class predisposition to it.

So he swam every week in a bid to be healthy, walked everywhere, and looked after himself as best he could. He lived kindly, and encouraged us to do the same.

In the car, the song continued:

'Doing the garden, digging the weeds.'

All four of us in the vegetable patch, a spring evening, 1992.

In 1635, John Taylor recorded the story of Old Tom Parr in his pamphlet, *The Old Man OR, The Age and long Life of Thomas Parr, the Son of John Parr of Winnington, in the Parish of Alberbury; in the County of Salop (or Shropshire) who was Borne in the Raigne of King Edward the 4th being aged 152 yeares and odd Monethes.* Old Tom married at eighty, had two children who did not survive childhood, and during his second marriage at one-hundred-and-five years old, had an affair with a woman called Katherine Milton. She bore his child out of wedlock and Parr was punished by being made to stand in a sheet in the porch of Alderbury Church during a particularly rainy time of the year.

'When your lights have gone.'

In January 1742, a man named Bright died aged one hundred-and-five, 'who had his memory and eyesight to the last insomuch as he could discern to pick a pin off the ground.' A lifelong resident of Shropshire, he was called the 'Second Old Parr'. Fifty-six years later, William Hyde died in his cottage on the slopes of Clee, 'in the 106th year of his age, and to the last moment in the full use of every faculty'.

'At one time, every seventh and every ninth year in a man's life was believed to bring great change and great dangers,' reports Christina Hole in her *Encyclopaedia of Superstitions*. 'Sixty-three, which is seven multiplied by nine, was therefore the most perilous of all ages, and if a man survived his sixty-third year, he might hope to live to a good old age.'

'Yours sincerely, wasting away.'

Mum started the car, and I turned off the radio. Outside the car, the changeable weather made trees shed petals and swayed the grass and twigs.

Six
A Shropshire Lad

MY HOUSE (MY BEDROOM)

OUR WORKROOM (MY HOUSE contd.)

Our workroom is a medium sized room with a
can carpet and light-blue walls. As you come in, on the left
is a blue table. Is our cupboard. For the size our positioned randomly are
two chairs. On the far side of the room is a window. The window is
a bit like the french windows (see louvre description) only they
don't quite touch the floor. Above the left hand side of the room
is a set of cupboards and shelves
Also made from blue) is one of
the shelves is a 4 ft-ft system.

<u>Simons Room (My House contd.)</u>

My brothers room is quite a large room; it is painted a very light
blue (Like my room) and has a window on the right. The window is
covered with light grey curtains. The room is a square shape. His
bed is positioned on the same wall as you come in. By his bed is
a dark brown chipboard cupboard. Above that is a black framed
mirror. To the left of that is his cupboard. Inside the cupboard
is a clothes rail and shelves to either side take the bottom left
for the passage-door. On the far wall is his desk . It is a black
desk with a light on it. Further on is a elm 3 shelved bookcase.

Beep beep sleep
Sleep Sleep
knock knock
"Time to wake up!"
Open eyes
(In doorway, Dad)
"It's a lovely day
for the race!"
He says.
"What race?"
(eyes rubbed)

Tracks and Traces

Watching wild animals requires skill and care but will richly reward your efforts. One of the most satisfying aspects of studying animals in the wild is the detective work necessary for interpreting tracks, droppings and feeding traces. These will help you to learn the local behaviour of an animal or group of animals, and from this you may be able to find the best places from which to keep watch.

Tracks vary a great deal from species to species, and also in the individual animal. For example, a deer walking will leave a track showing the hind foot placed in the print of the fore foot. The faster the animal moves, the further in front of the fore foot goes the hind foot. If the animal leaps, then the small hind toes register as well as the hooves, and the hooves of the fore feet are splayed outwards.

Deer tracks

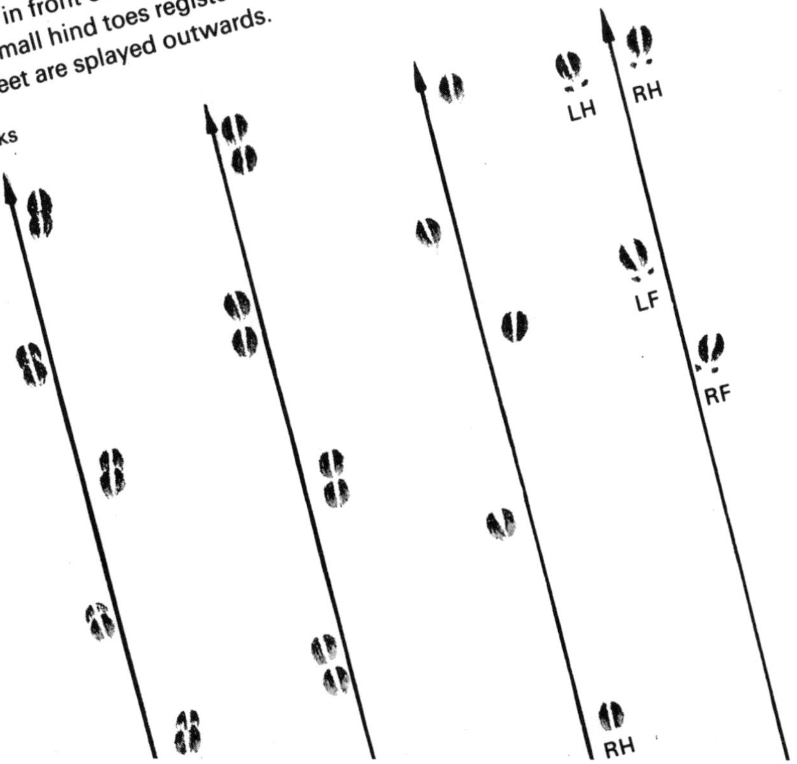

the fore on the other. Just change step and tu opposite side of th

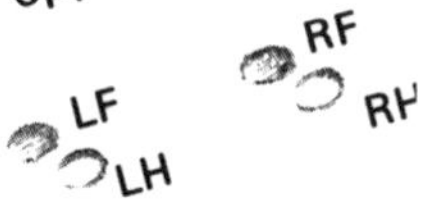

LF   RF
LH   RH

The Smallest

Shrews, mice keep away fro Field voles r droppings,

Jumpin

Rur

LH   RH

LF

RF

RH

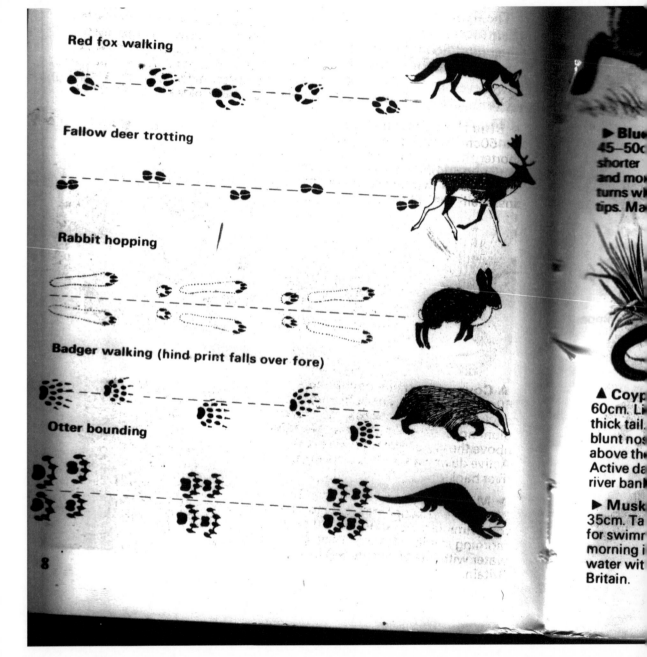

Red fox walking

Fallow deer trotting

Rabbit hopping

Badger walking (hind print falls over fore)

Otter bounding

8

▶ **Blue**
45–50c
shorter
and mor
turns wh
tips. Ma

▲ **Coyp**
60cm. Li
thick tail.
blunt nos
above the
Active da
river bank

▶ **Musk**
35cm. Ta
for swimm
morning i
water wit
Britain.

A SON OF THE SOIL

IF you take the first turning to the right and the second to the left down any country lane you will probably find the forgotten England—the rural England that has watched the mechanical majesty of the arterial road sweep past with all the calm of a sitting cat. You may find a village or a farm, or perhaps only a clog-maker's encampment, but nobody there would be really dismayed if all the wheels in creation stopped revolving. Most of us would have to live in abysmal darkness if the electric lights went out for ever; and not only would we be baffled by the _____ that turns heat into light, _____ not even know how to _____ ing oil to supply _____ Many of us, now _____ light, could no _____ oil lamp eff_____ things we _____ were other _____

Yet in _____ England _____

whom the elements of living simple as they are to any front___ There is nothing essential to th___ living that they would have to g___ if mass production ceased ___ They could feed themselves, cl___ selves, build their own houses ___ hundred and one jobs that we___ lot of pastoral men. And a ___ hands for them, they would ___ to add the _____ to that _____

_____ _____ _____ _____ _____ _____ now how _____ face of E _____ achieved by _____ same view as _____ likely that the _____ will see the same unc ___ hill and dale. And

... the rhythm of its seasons, ... part of them; they ... prepared to endure much for a little profit. They follow in the ways of a long line of grey ghosts, hardy pioneers who have been battling with great odds for centuries. It is from them that the countrymen of today—the dairyman, the shepherd, the ploughman, the cowman, the thatcher, the hurdle maker and their fellows—have developed a shrewdness. Even though they now handle machinery with the skilled fingers of mechanics, they still have the knack of handling animals, of reading weather signs, and of going about their craftsmen's tasks with that wise quietness that keeps you aware of their sound business instinct in not owning how good a time they have had since they were set down on earth.

the presence in the village of the fertilization spirit in the visible and tangible form of flowers and green foliage or of the fruits of the earth.

the aged thane of Caynham, his beard half-covering his flowing moss-green robe.

'We have ploughed and we have sowed,
We have reaped and we have mowed,
And we have brought home every load!
Hurrah for Harvest Home!'

As red as an apple, as round as a ball,
Higher than the steeple, weathercock and all.

the Dike lit wa...
black shapes, some squa...
...elms and sable shields. Hun...
...over the Dike and through the...
...e walls from cliff to cliff. Thund...
...ing...own.
...in ...me whistling over the battlem...
...ng ...the stones. Some found...
...p had ...un, but no sound or cha...
...ering arro...came.
...s halted, foiled by the silent menac...
...gain the lightning...e aside the da...
...aving sper...nd...sword, and s...

Wednesday 16th February

...not a happy place

School is not always a Happy
Place.

Bullies about, ouch that hurt me

School is not a happy place when
that happens
Tom, stop that kicking, Bob stop
that
Pow, punch, kick, ouch stop that
Martin
The playground is like a battle
field
wah, wah, wah what's the

Seven
A reminder

'This is the sort of lad we want'

The
G

INDUSTRY WELCOMES PRODUCTS OF F.B.C. TRAINING SCHEME

L EADERSHIP and character training organised by the Birmingham Federation of Boys Clubs is paying such big dividends that local industrialists are urging the federation to increase the scope of its training courses.

They find that boys who have spent their week-ends climbing mountains in the dark, canoeing and studying archæology are more reliable when it comes to working in a factory.

Mr. John Carney-Smith, an advertising executive who has been helping the federation for some years, has been appointed to organise a fund-raising campaign to enable more boys to be sent on week-end courses at Nash Court in the Clee Hills.

Mr. Paul Winterforde-Young, secretary of the federation, said yesterday: "At present we can only send away 40 boys for a week-end once a month, and we could not do that if the Education Authority did not meet a third of the cost."

At Nash Court groups of seven or eight boys are dropped out on the Clee Hills or the Long Mynd after dark and left to trek across dangerous country to a given point.

When they return they are awarded marks for observation, punctuality, camping methods—and even for the way they present their reports.

WITH CRAFTSMEN

On other occasions they are sent out to spend the day with local craftsmen or at places of architectural or archæological interest.

"One firm, right outside Birmingham, has recognised the value of this type of training and ___ ___ ___ enthusiastic that they

THE 'GLOBE TROTTING RECTOR' IS OFF AGAIN

Canon Green leaves for South Africa tomorrow

O NCE again the label-plastered bags of Canon Bryan Green are r e a d y packed. Birmingham's "globe trotting rector" is off to South Africa tomorrow. This latest trip will bring the total journeys of Britain's most travelled clergyman close to a record 250,000 miles.

Since he came to Birmingham six years ago, Canon Green, who has been described as "one of the best evangelists in the Anglican church," has visited all five continents at least once. He has preached in Ceylon and Honolulu, New Zealand and America.

Some people have been critical of his many long absences from his parish which, they suggested, was being neglected.

"There has been some talk," admitted Canon Green yesterday, "but most people are very pleased. My congregation certainly is.

For two months

"St Martin's doesn't suffer. There is the lecturer and three curates to carry on when I am not there."

There had been more criticism when he was vicar at Holy ___ — London's

SHOW TITLE FOR MISS PALETHORPE

M ISS DAWN PALE-THORPE, aged 19, of Blakedown, Kidderminster, became women's show jumping champion at the White City International Horse Show last night when she won the Queen Elizabeth II Cup, open for competition to women riders of any nationality.

She rode Earlsrath Rambler.

Equal second were Mrs. Brian Marshall, wife of a National Hunt jockey, on Nobbler, and Miss Susan Whitehead, on Eforeglot.

Miss Pat Smythe was unlucky when her horse Prince Hal refused at one jump and unseated his rider. She clung to the reins for half a minute while she struggled to regain the saddle, but finally had to fall, sustaining 21 faults, which eliminated her.

MINISTER 'OPEN' D___ ON FR___

D IGBETH—Birmingham's ___ artery—will be closed to ___ Friday, while it is officially ___ Transport, Mr. J. Boyd-Carper___

The £1m. double-lane highw___ after Birmingham Corporation ___ years for permission to widen ___ ___ Digbeth and Deritend ___

An indifferent salutation

On October 20 1764, 'a bailiff who went to arrest a collier in the pits on the Clee hills was killed by the said collier, who has since been apprehended and committed to Shrewsbury Gaol; as have likewise four other colliers who were spectators of the murder.'

'For three quarters of an hour,' in September of 1880, 'a fearful fight took place in the turnpike on the Clee Hills, in which all the parties were concerned, and culminated in a regular riot, some hundreds of people being on the ground. Most disgraceful fighting took place in the presence of the policeman, who did his best to prevent the rioting, but was threatened with violence if he interfered.' Benjamin Hammond, Peter Pope, Thomas Williams, William Robinson, Andrew Williams, James Benbow, Thomas Beddoe and George Williams were charged with breaching the peace on Titterstone Clee; Edmund Wilkinson was charged with aiding and abetting. George Williams and Thomas Beddoe were also charged with assault.

In November 1883, 'a race of novel character came off at Clee Hill between C. Tanzy, alias "Jumbo" and R. Parry, alias "The Goat", the former to run 50 yards carrying a man on his back, against the latter running 100 yards. After a very exciting race "Jumbo" was hailed the winner by two yards.'

In 1955, the Birmingham Federations of Boys Clubs appointed a Mr John Carney-Smith, an advertising executive, to organise a fund-raising campaign to 'enable more boys to be sent on weekend courses at Nash Court.' Groups of seven or eight boys would be dropped out on the Clee Hills after dark and left, 'to trek across dangerous country to a given point.'

'When they return,' continues the *Birmingham Daily Gazette*, 'they are awarded marks for observation, punctuality, camping methods – and even for the way they present their reports.'

In January 1956, local farmers and an RSPCA inspector failed in their attempts to capture a young, half-wild pony that was roaming Titterstone with a tin can stuck on its foot. The pony had been spotted by motorists on Clee Hill Common. The plan was to return to the hill when the light improved, and entice an older, tamer pony first, and use that as a lure to bring the injured pony to them. Around the same time, it was reported, sheep had been stealing sandwiches from picnickers on the hill.

I once met an artist from Coventry who told me how he used to go walking on Titterstone Clee while a pupil at the City of Coventry Boarding School at Cleobury Mortimer. The school was established in 1939 as Wyre Farm Camp in response to the National Camps Corporation's efforts to create schools and educational camps for city children and evacuees. It was purchased by Coventry Local Education Authority in 1957 and became a secondary modern boarding school.

The artist had been sent there from Coventry for reasons that he did not elaborate on. He told me he would walk for miles up Clee Hill in search of cigarettes, delinquent, and how it was the time at which the 'Black Panther' Donald Neilson was at large and everyone on the hill was scared and curtain-twitching. Neilson was a prolific burglar whose crimes had turned violent, killing three Post Office workers in three raids across the country in 1973. On 14 January 1975, Neilson broke into the Shropshire home of George Whittle, owner of Go Whittle, whose coaches shipped us around as schoolchildren. Neilson kidnapped their daughter, Lesley, and held her captive on a ledge in a drainage shaft in Staffordshire, a noose around her neck. He made ransom demands which the family attempted to meet, but Neilson fled when the handover failed. Lesley Whittle was found dead on 7 March 1975; she had slipped, or was pushed, from the ledge she occupied and had been hanged.

Neilson was captured in December 1975 and received five life sentences for

Whittle's murder and the murder of the Post Office workers, and a further sixty-one years for his other crimes of extortion, assault and kidnap. He died on 18 December 2011 after being transferred from Norwich Prison to Norfolk and Norwich University Hospital suffering from breathing difficulties.

In 1983 on Titterstone Clee, 'the charred bodies of salesman Mike Naylor, his wife Jean, and teenage children Mark and Sarah, were found lying side by side on the floor of the secluded home they chose as refuge from the hectic West Midlands.'

Down the hill, Castle Hill School opened a couple of years later. Ralph Morris, the headteacher, had inflated his own credentials after leaving a post at nearby Nash Court School in order to establish Castle Hill. He quickly established a terrible pyramid of abuse, manipulating the boys in his care – many of them extraordinarily troubled – into closely patrolled teams of violent enforcement, victims turned victors by cash and cigarettes, a 'highly sophisticated network of corruption ... so effective and at the same time so infectious that these boys were afraid to complain,' as a report by Shropshire County Council later described it.

After a number of mishandled complaints, including ignored testimony from boys who spoke out – many of whom recanted their statements after Morris was allowed to speak with them – a case was finally brought against him. On 12 April 1991, he was sentenced at Shrewsbury Crown Court to twelve years' imprisonment for sixteen offences against young people in his care, including physical, indecent and sexual assault and rape; he was understood to have sexually and physically abused over ninety boys in his care over a nearly ten-year period. He died in his cell at Littlehey Prison, Cambridgeshire in 1996, from a perforated stomach after eating metal items – screws, batteries, drawing pins and razors.

In August 2016, aged thirty-three, someone I knew from the village school died after a short illness. I met him when we were ten. He was very friendly. I have a clear memory of him on a Go Whittle coach when we were going somewhere – probably to the swimming pool in Ludlow. He had a cassette of 'Elegant Slumming' by M People for his Walkman. I didn't have a Walkman, and all my parents' cassettes were home-dubbed, so it was the first time I'd seen a professionally printed cassette. He liked football and looked after me. He smiled a lot. I hadn't seen him in twenty-five years, and I thought of him only occasionally in that time. I doubt he ever thought about me.

And so on.

I was thinking about all of this one day while driving home to Bristol from Manchester. We had been stuck in a traffic jam, watching a man in his camper van feed water to his dog from a plastic shoe, waiting for the cars to move. The traffic unclogged, and a few exultant miles later, I saw it. We were just south of Bromsgrove on the M5.

I had never twigged before that you would be able to see it from the motorway, but there it was, across the other side of the carriageway, fuzzy in the summer heat, just on the horizon, like a big, looming, ambivalent statement, like an indifferent salutation saying, what can you even remember about me? Does your story even matter?

Eight
Hope

You want to go out Friday

A few days later, Tim flew in from San Francisco.
Dad's condition had stabilised. Tim spoke with the doctors and nurses and occupational health – he has always been good at this stuff, the practical, the detail, the scientific – and Dad was able to come home.

Ali and I waited at my parents' house for a large, full boy of kind, dry humour and computer-gamer eyes to deliver, unload and assemble a hospital bed. A downstairs room became Dad's makeshift ward. We spruced the room up as best we could, but that hospital bed was a big, ugly, adjustable whale that just screamed 'illness'.

Later that day, Mum and Tim brought Dad home. Ignoring me, he moved straight to Ali to give her a hug.

'Most important person first,' he said. We laughed.

Dad had been given a set of crutches. The doctors were concerned about the integrity of his hip and his delicate femur, both of which had been affected by the spreading cancer. The osteologists were talking about hip replacements, while the oncologists were more concerned about the strength he'd need for his treatment. The competing priorities of the specialists stirred in us a sense of dissonance. Was Dad's prognosis positive enough to warrant considering surgery for a new hip? Were they expecting him to live that long? Weeks? Months? Years? That's not what we thought the biopsies were saying. Perhaps we had misunderstood.

No clear answer was forthcoming, but Dad, being game for most things and having an unerring faith in medical knowledge, happily acquiesced. During his time at home, he took great care practising on the crutches. He gleefully hobbled around. We laughed gently at him as he counted out the rhythm to get the left left right left left right correct. He feigned offence at our teasing and challenged us to have a go for ourselves. I, particularly, failed miserably.

In this way, the crutches in that moment provided us with a few little moments of levity in a process largely devoid of laughs. We learned to take these little pearls – clouded by the million 'what ifs?' that were constantly being calculated by our anxious brains – and make whatever bizarre necklace we could with them, so that they became these little stars, glimmering in the gloom.

That evening, Ali and I cooked dinner for everyone, and we all sat around the table together. Dad was delighted at this rare chance for my brother and I to be in the same place at the same time. Dad managed a glass of red wine. He went to bed early. So did we, exhausted.

The next day, Ali and I returned to Bristol in a light flurry of snow, back to work, to feed the cat and try and carry on as normally as we could. My brother stayed on in Devon, helping Mum with the new regime of pills, and the technicalities and practicalities of caring for someone who is ill.

With Dad stable, and plans being made for treatment, Tim reluctantly went back to California a week later. We were all still frantic, but allowed ourselves to think that it might be OK.

Nine
Holy Hills
Pt. 2

The same river

September 2018. I'm driving on the road from Callow Hill to Cleobury Mortimer when a little tawny face, soft and startled, appears ahead of my car. My hands clench and my teeth crackle.

'Shit,' I say to myself. 'Shit shit shit.'

The pheasant makes a dull and perversely underwhelming thud as her death vibrates up through my seat and into my own body. I drive on, biting my lip and looking-not-looking in the rear-view mirror.

'Shit shit shit.'

When I was about nine years old, one of our cats caught a mouse. When he left it quivering on the grizzly bristles of the mat by the backdoor, I insisted that it be me that put the rodent out of its misery; I really don't know why – probably trying to be a grown up, and death and mercy seemed pretty grown up – and I don't know why Mum or Dad acquiesced, either. I moved the mouse to the lawn and picked up a trowel. I struck the animal once, but the blow was too nervously delivered to kill. I hit the mouse again, faster and harder, fuelled by a strange panic that tasted like metal; it wasn't done. I struck it again, with a force that felt utterly excessive.

I looked down at the tiny, fish-boned croquette of warm fur in the grass and began to cry. I sobbed rivers and waterfalls. I shook like gorse flowers in the wind, or a fly stuck in a cobweb. I drank in the walnut tree and mud smell of the garden in my snotty sniffs. I heard my Dad saying soothing things. I looked at the small dead mouse, and wondered, 'Will I ever be forgiven for what I have done?'

I arrive at Titterstone Clee Hill a little while later. I inspect the bumper and find no evidence of what has happened.

I leave the car park, walking away from Titterstone Clee's dome-like summit – they reckon the name Clee comes from *cleo* or *cleowe*, Old English for a 'ball-shaped massif' – and Dad's radars.

As I make my way down the single-track road I hear the sound of water. I step off the tarmac and down a slope to investigate.

Just beneath the level of the road a stream emerges from a drainage tunnel. I consult my map. It is called Benson's Brook. I crouch down and poke around with bare fingers in the very brisk stream. My feet sink in the mud. The water goes from left to right in a delicate, tinkling flow. It shines glossily over dark rocks sat in sediment the blood-brown colour of a pheasant's plumage.

I climb up the opposite bank and look around. The drizzle and September cloud makes it feel like I'm viewing the world through spectacles greasy with breakfast fingerprints, which I probably am. Dad used to wash his glasses every morning. I'd watch him over my breakfast, his shape against the window above the sink. It was a quiet little ritual, delicately sluicing away the previous day's grime with a dash of washing-up liquid. Mum says he gave up this habit almost as soon as he retired.

Taking leave of the road, I pick out a sheep path and follow it northeast through the rough grasses of the wastes. Crunching over the ear-waxy sepia lobes of mysterious fungi, which my book tells me might be false chanterelles, I disturb a little shoal of birds and they levitate suddenly, sounding like distressed bicycle wheels.

I skirt Folly Well, a boggy patch of land where Benson Brook rises. As I head onwards, the brook flows away from me, back down the hill, through ten feet of concrete tunnel under the road, where it emerges at the other side of the culvert, indifferent to my rapidly drowning footprints.

Next, the brook flows west, growing in stature, through Horseditch and Nine Spring Covert. By Bedlam it moves through a silted-up reservoir and vaguely recalls a previous life as it sends itself over a small, narrow dam. Constructed between 1883 and 1885 by Field and Mackay, the dam was allegedly part of one of the very first hydroelectric installations in the world. They used it to power either a quarry's stone-crushers, before they were moved further up Titterstone, or the lights on an industrial incline railway to Bitterley – nobody's quite sure which.

The water, unfazed by this pedigree, blithely flows on, away from the dam and down the slope, until it finds its way first into Bitterley Brook, then Dogditch Brook, and then into the Ledwyche. The Ledwyche then makes its way towards Caynham, where it curls around the northern slopes of Caynham Camp, before turning roughly due south, following a road called The Sheet.

On a bend in a wooded valley there is a small stone bridge perpendicular to the road which carries a narrow lane up to Poughnhill farm and Caynham Cottage. It was at this bridge that Mr George Berney Charleton, tenant at Caynham Cottage, nearly met his maker on August 7 1894. 'Mr G. B. Charleton and a lady friend were returning from the sale of work at Caynham Court,' reported the *Ludlow Advertiser*; 'Mr Charleton was driving, and the night being dark, the pony ... turned too short and went into the river. Mr Charleton was driven into the water but managed to escape without injury. His friend by catching hold of some boughs of a tree extricated herself from the conveyance ... The pony was drowned.'

We once went to a party at Caynham Cottage, sometime in late 1993 or early 1994. I'm fairly sure of the date because the daughter of the farmer who threw the party was a classmate at the Caynham village school, to which I had just moved after the bullying in Ludlow became too acute. It was also cold, and as we had left Shropshire by the summer of 1994, that narrowed the timeframe to the winter months.

At the party, something was starting, a sense of electricity, magnetism, excited at togetherness with new friends, and the recklessness of being up past my bedtime. The parents talked and we ran around. Was it bonfire night?

Sixteen years after his accident, Charleton dropped down dead, maybe where the crisps and snacks were laid out, while making a speech to commemorate the opening of a new parish room, on January 4 1911. He was attended by a local physician, but nothing could be done.

The funeral took place three days later at Caynham, and according to the *Tenbury Wells Advertiser* was held, 'amidst manifest signs of regret. There were close on four hundred present, representative of the nobility, landed gentry and farmers, etc, of the neighbourhood.'

I didn't know any of this in 1993, of course. Instead, I was preoccupied by the fact that there were outdoor spotlights in the flower beds. Who has spotlights in their garden? That's weird. We didn't. But then we didn't live on a farm, and my Dad didn't drop me off at school in his tractor.

I pressed my gloved hand against the glass screen of the light and left behind a nylon melted five-finger paw print. Light bulbs were hot! What a thing to learn!

At some point, two new friends, brothers, suggested a sleepover at their house. The new school was teaching me about other people, about how not to hide, about the matter-of-fact, shoulder-shrugging kindness of my new peers. I approached my mum, nervously wiggling; I assumed that because I was about to circumvent the usual protocol for organising a sleepover – 'I'll get my mum to ring your mum' – this wasn't going to work.

'Muuuum... Mum, can I ummm you know Ben and I...' I whined.

My mum, sensing what was happening, interrupted. 'No need for a silly voice,' she said kindly, 'just ask.'

I fidgeted. I was ten years old, five years older than Anthony Curtis, son of a later owner of Caynham Court, was when he slipped into the weir one hundred and twenty metres downstream of Caynham Cottage on the first day of February 1943, and drowned.

'Can I stay over at Ben and Jamie's?'

On Tuesday December 4 1888, a man called James Williams was walking towards Ludlow, when he saw Silas Harris, fifty-eight years of age, jump into the Ledwyche a little further downstream from the weir. Unable to help, Williams watched in vain as Harris was carried away. His body was recovered after an hour and a half of searching.

His daughter Margaret had written to her Aunt and Uncle the morning before he died, and she read her letter at the coroner's inquest.

'He has been going into melancholy,' she recounted. 'We have tried all we can to cheer him but it is of no use… We are all nearly broken-hearted and scarcely know what to be doing.'

'Of course. Let's find their mum and dad.'

Below us, the Ledwyche slinked its way through the countryside and through my childhood, before emptying into the Teme, and then the Severn, and then the Bristol Channel, before coming back as rain where it all started, a reminder that, as Heraclitus once said, 'You can never step in the same river twice.'

'Heraclitus, I believe, says that all things go and nothing stays,' remarked Plato, 'and comparing existence to the flow of a river, he says you could not step twice into the same river.' Another translation credits Heraclitus as saying, 'on those stepping into rivers staying the same, other and other waters flow'; that is the river remains a river, and in its permanence, it allows other things to change. At the same time, it changes, too: its course, its nature, its volume. Similarly, we change as people, but we are the same people, too; 'we both step and do not step in the same rivers. We are and are not.'

I'm fairly sure I don't understand Heraclitus fully, but still the hill feels like what I think he's describing – always the same, but always different, always changing and shifting, both there and not there; it reminds me that things are always changing, and it is always changing to remind me it has always been the same.

When I step on these slopes, I suffer the same fate, both here and not here, both new and old, the same and different.

Cole, lyme, yren and stone

I carry on wading through the tussocks of sheep-shorn bilberry bushes, thick, heathy grasses, and lichens.

Titterstone has long been the focus of human industry. Leland writes that there is 'no great Plenty of Wood in Cle Hills, yet ther is sufficient Brushe wood. Plenty of Cole Yerth Stone nether exceding good for Lyme, whereof there they make muche and serve the centre about.' There's not really any part of Titterstone Clee that hasn't somehow been scooped, smoothed, cut, soothed, scraped or marked by the extraction of all this stuff.

I'm walking now on the common land, which covers around 2,108 acres but likely covered more in mediaeval years. I'm looking for signs of human activity. It's not hard to find – you can see the evidence in the great grassy barrows of spoil tips, the raw cliff faces, submerged pits, strange lumps, tumbled walls, abandoned kilns, railway tracks and disused buildings, from the outlines of missing mediaeval squatters' cottages, to the still-standing terraces erected later to house labourers and their families.

Just west of the radar station, I come across the remains of a coal-mining bell pit. These were shallow excavations, with vertical shafts sunk to access the coal seams that lay close to the surface. The spoil was mounded around the opening, giving a sort of doughnut appearance. When a pit was exhausted, the farmers would move a few feet away and begin again. These clusters are visible today on aerial photographs: little rings with dark centres.

I sit down on its raised bank. Saplings and long green stems thrive in its centre.

I see a little bit of coal at my feet. I pick it up. I wonder where this bit has come from after all this time.

After a short rest, I carry on walking in search of evidence of settlement. The regional population grew notably in the sixteenth and seventeenth centuries, thanks largely to migration to the area to take advantage of the common land. This intensified the activity on the hills, including squatting – building homes on the common land that became permanent – and digging not only for coal, but also for clay to produce pipes, domestic earthenware and bricks.

Clay was dug from pits, and processed on a small scale in farms and households. Items were fired in beehive kilns and in domestic fires, often glazed with a dark, shiny slip. Some of the older farms further down the hill still have these kilns on their land.

Lime was made from the sedimentary limestone that lay below Clee's igneous cap and on its slopes. It was used variously as a soil improver in agriculture, a disinfectant for white-washing walls, and in building mortar. It was also used in the production of iron; in Leland's time, there were 'Blo Shopps to make yren apon the Ripes or Bankes of Mylbroke, comynge out of Caderton Cle or Casset Wood.'

Lime burners acquired a reputation for deviousness, or perhaps, opportunistic behaviour, so much so that 'to come limer over' became a phrase in the local dialect, meaning to dupe or take advantage. It was explained to folklorist Charlotte Burne by reference to the following example, recorded in her three-volume work, *Shropshire Folk-lore; A Sheaf of Gleanings*: 'Three lime-burners goo to a public for some yale, two young uns an' an owd un; the owd un tak's car' to sit i' the middle, so as the jug posses backerts an' forrats e' gets as much agen drink as the young uns.'

During the eighteenth and nineteenth centuries, coal mining intensified. Before that period, while some landowners levied charges from tenants to extract coal and there was some taxation – the earliest reference to coal mining on Titterstone Clee comes from the 1291 *Taxatio Ecclesiastica* of Pope Nicholas IV which lists profits derived by Wigmore Abbey from the sale of Titterstone coal – mostly communities were left to mine for their own subsistence. However, as industrialisation intensified and the demand for coal grew, larger pits – like Top Trout, Bottom Trout and Barn

Pit – were sunk to access the deeper coal seams.

'Drilling through the hard rock,' writes Kenneth Goodman in his 1978 PhD thesis *Hammerman's Hill: the Land, People and Industry of Titterstone Clee Hill Area of Shropshire from the Sixteenth to the Eighteenth Centuries*, 'was a very difficult and expensive task. It required a great amount of capital and good fortune for there was little knowledge either of the thickness of the basalt, which could vary from forty to three hundred feet, or of the position and depth of seams. At Titterstone Quarry the basalt rests immediately above the Great Coal sea, but northeast of Cornbrook it is one hundred and eighty feet above it.'

Sinking a shaft involved a laborious process using hammers, chisels and flattened rods called 'feathers' to crack through the sill. The shafts, once sunk, relied on men to hew at the face, while coal was shifted away in sledges called 'carvs', drawn by the shoulders of young boys, known as 'donkeys'. The coal was unloaded by bucket and winched up at the pit head.

Women would then carry the coal down the hill in sacks across their backs to where merchant carts would collect the material. There's a rock nearby, called the Stooping Stone, where the women would rest their loads on their way down the hill; at the bottom the coal was loaded on to a horse and cart for market.

The process changed once more when the Titterstone and Dhustone incline railways were opened in the mid-nineteenth century. The two lines, which included a system of ropes and pulleys to move carts up and down, met at Bitterley, where the line connected with the main railway to take coal to Ludlow. Bitterley itself acquired a grim reputation, perhaps owing to the intense and constant work happening in the yards there. It was remembered in a Shropshire rhyme,

'Bitterley, Bitterley, under the Clee
Devil take me if ever come to thee.'

It was the advent of industrial quarrying that had perhaps the biggest impact on the communities, landscapes and language of Titterstone and the Clee Hills. Clee stone, known locally as dhustone, is blue-grey-black and hard as hammers, with a toughness and character that, suggests Grenville A. J. Cole in his 1921 book *Common Stones; Unconventional Essays in Geology*, 'brings us into touch with the grim recesses of the earth.' Cole goes on to describe how, 'in its undecomposed condition, dolerite makes an ideal metal for the roads. It does not powder down like granite, and it is, on the other hand, tough rather than hard and flinty.'

The Dhustone Quarry opened on Clee Hill in 1863, initially to service a contract to pave Cardiff Docks. The material, however, was tough to extract. The earliest technique for separating rock from the quarry face was to light fires against the exposed dhustone, then douse the flames with water to make the whole contract suddenly. While effective, this produced unstable cliff faces, many of which still mark the surface of the hill. The dhustone blocks that came down could be further cracked by fires set overnight, but mostly the work was achieved by labour with large hammers.

The stone would be further broken into smaller cubes, called setts, that were finished by hand knapping. Chisels couldn't be used as their points would blunt too readily. Instead the sett makers would hold a sett in one hand, and strike its edges with a set of dressing hammers, turning the piece as they went.

In 1881 Field and MacKay opened Titterstone Quarry, and the neighbouring East Quarry in 1910. The works, which at their peak shifted 400,000 tonnes a year, have taken a great bite from the southern reaches of the summit.

The Magpie Quarry opened on Clee Hill's eastern slopes around 1904, overlooking Catherton Common. The stone from this site was transported on a demented ski lift, with giant buckets hung along a loop of steel cable, seven miles long and three and a half inches thick, that ran at a height of over forty feet.

It operated at five miles per hour, moving one tonne per minute, driven by a winching station at the Magpie Quarry. The stone was loaded and unloaded by hand at the railway station at Detton Ford, on the Cleobury Mortimer and Ditton Priors Light Railway.

One testament to the disruption of the industry is traced in the names on Clee. A string of houses built along the Titterstone incline became known as Bedlam. In his memoir, *Titterstone Clee, Everyday Life, Industrial History and Dialect*, Alf Jenkins reports how it was the noise of quarrying and the constant push and pull of the carts on the railway that gave it the name, but also recounts an earlier rumour: 'in the early 1920s, when a Mr. Aves was head of Bitterley Grammar School, he stated that if you walked from Titterstone Cottages towards the hilltop, through the common gate, you soon arrived at the end of enclosed land. If you turned left and continued along the common land hedge, it was possible to find the remains of ... a hospital for those with disturbed minds. The wailing and anxious cries from this establishment created bedlam and this is the source of the continued nickname.'

Another impact of the new industry was the emergence of a distinctive dialect spoken only on the Clees. It came into being only briefly, lasting in common use for barely one hundred years before evolving away.

While the distinctive – and regionally varied – Shropshire vocabulary had drawn the attention of folklorists and 'collectors' like Georgia F. Jackson, who in 1879 produced the *Shropshire Word-book: A Glossary Of Archaic And Provincial Words, Etc.,* the Clee dialect was a mixture of more national vocabularies.

Quarrymen worked in dangerous conditions, in fog and mist and wind and sun, for long hours, for little pay. But it was skilled and labour-intensive work, and people began to move across the country to work in the quarries. The dialect emerged in the mid to late eighteenth century from the mixture of accents and dialects that came together during this emigration, not just from neighbouring Wales and the Midlands, whose vocabularies already coloured the border dialect, but also from as far afield as Nottinghamshire, Yorkshire, Lancashire, Tyneside, Scotland and Cornwall.

The communities on the top of the Clee hills remained isolated from the nearby towns and villages thanks to both a lack of infrastructure and aggressive weather. This meant that long days spent in one another's company, working and resting, became a crucible for the evolution a new way of speaking.

The speech – recordings of which still exist – took the rounded, sing-song patterns of the Shropshire accent, lengthened some vowels, shortened others, and added new twists and turns. Sentences flowed unctuously before dropping into a staccato of clipped syllables, then carrying on again, swooping like the hills' ring ouzels.

Jenkins, whose memoir contains a glossary of Clee words and phrases, says that the dialect was completely alien to those living at the base of the hill, and that he himself was teased at school in Ludlow for speaking it. The dialect lasted into the middle of the twentieth century, fading as two wars, new technologies and increasingly inaccessible raw materials led to the decline of the hill's industries, and the dispersal of many of the communities.

While I'm out exploring, one phrase for a wayfaring practice sticks out, literally and figuratively, material evidence of which is still visible in the earth around the hill. Travelling to and from the hill for work often happened when it was so dark 'tha kood nu sa,' either under the racket of the dawn chorus, or in the gloaming at twilight. No matter how well-worn the paths, without streetlights it was easy to get lost in all the hedgerows and fields and ditches and brooks as the land rose up towards the Clees. The solution was for the commuters to drop pieces of broken crockery, 'pitch-uck', as they went. This breadcrumb trail, crunchy under foot, or glinting in the morning or the moonlight, or shining pale against the midnight-blue of the grass or dirt of the track, would illuminate their route, like little stars.

Newfound Well

About five hundred metres north-northeast of the bell pit are the remnants of Newfound Well Farm, 'a gaunt-looking ruined dwelling house amidst windswept trees', as an article in the *Shrewsbury Chronicle* described it in the winter of 1957.

I find my way there along the remains of a path which is still a little dented from carriage wheels. The ruins sit in an enclosure, bounded by toppling drystone walls. There's a modern gate, tied to two iron poles, and a hollow-trunked sweet chestnut tree, spiky with nuts, next to it. The tree looks surprisingly old, with a low, wide canopy. The big leaves are a striking green, and droop all the way to the earth. On the bare ground beneath, thinned by sheep, the ground is piebald with shiny, inky-black dung. There are two other trees nearby, brittle and grey as tombstones, one ash, one lime.

I climb over the gate, which has been painted blue. Ahead of me, the footprint of the building is unmistakable, two rooms divided by a corridor with two smaller spaces, all marked out in thick blocks of Clee stone. The walls still stand to a height of at least two or three feet, higher in some places. Banks of earth, full of voids and demolition rubble, broken tile, all covered in a thin turf, soften the edges, so it looks a bit like the walls are teeth peering out of the gummy earth. Amongst the demolition rubble old locally made bricks float up, looking like marble cake.

I sit on a wall, next to a finger of stone that was once the northeast corner of the farmhouse. There's a clear view of Brown Clee to the north. Behind me, in the corner of the enclosure are what at first I take to be outhouses, but are in fact something quite different.

Around August 1840, the farm opened up access to the waters that sprang up in its enclosure. 'The spring, though thus named, has been long known for its efficacy, and in some instances for the cure of different diseases,' reported the *Worcester Chronicle* that year. 'It possesses the same qualities and purity as the waters of Malvern and the proprietor has lately enclosed the spring within a small building, but the public have access to it free of expense. A bath, also enclosed, has been constructed by the proprietor, which may be used without any remuneration to himself, but the person who has the care and cleans the bath and building will be entitled to threepence each time from any one who bathes, except the very poor, from whom there will not be any payment required.'

Whether or not it really did have a reputation as a healing spring before it became open to the public, I don't know, but the apparent lack of a profit motive seems to suggest that maybe it was a genuine belief on the hill.

I root around in the foundations of the remaining outhouses. There's a well – or maybe a drain – its opening a square of red brick in a tumble of drystone walling and lumps of lime whitewash. The bathing rooms sit next door, the faint slope down into the waters still discernible. There's a cistern of some kind further up the slope with a tree growing from it. The spring itself gurgles just below, lost in nettles and bracken.

The farm started life as a squatters' cottage, enclosed on the common land outside of the parish boundaries. By the nineteenth century, it was functioning as a tree plantation – at Christmas in 1835, fifty oak trees and one hundred-and-four ash trees grown on the site were auctioned. The owners also reared sheep – a report in 1904 describes Charles Millichamp losing 'a Welsh ewe and a lamb' from the farm.

Diversification of this kind was pretty commonplace. Life on the hill for these communities was not easy, and poverty and illness were rampant. Working conditions were harsh and dangerous in the industries and settlements were often isolated from the larger villages lower down the hill by a lack of roads and the bad weather; some farms could be snowed in for months on end during the winter.

Well into the twentieth century most families had small holdings. Hill stock – stubbly sheep, rarely cattle – was sold at winter, before the hills became too cold for the animals to survive. Pigs were also valuable, fed scraps and slaughtered in any month with an a 'r' in it for bacon, sausage and chitterlings. Whole families worked, whether on the quarries, in the kilns, and at the lime pits, in the mines, bringing in the crops for local farmers, mucking out the pigs, or feeding the chickens in the evenings. After the harvest, women and children would walk the fields, picking the stubble for stray bits of corn with which to make bread.

As with many other rural communities, days on the hills were experienced through the push and pull of Christianity, tempered by superstition, folklore and the rhythm of life established by the quietude. A vicar on the Clee hills, upon planning a sermon preaching against the belief in witchcraft, 'was dissuaded from doing so by the parish schoolmaster, who assured him that the belief was so deeply rooted in the people's minds that he would be more likely to alienate them from the Church than to weaken their faith in witchcraft.'

In 1843 Burne collected a story from a man on the hill that echoes these beliefs. 'A waggoner w'en a went to sup up, used to fine 'is 'orses in a lather. 'E couldna mak out whad wuz the raison. Soo a wentun to a wise-man, an' 'er toud 'im to watch, for it wuz the witch as wuz ridin' 'em; soo a watched an' watched, but a sid nuthin, an' the 'orses wun i' the same fettle every night. But at last a sid a bit o' straw a-top on one o' thar necks, an' soo a laid out on it, an' took it, an' sed some charm the man 'ad touden 'im. An' then a chucked it o' the fire, and the owd witch wuz sid gwine up the chimdy on a broomstick.'

The moralising crusade of the church was not, however, stayed; in 1836 a fundraising campaign began 'to erect a chapel on that part of the Titterstone Clee Hill, which is thickly inhabited by persons employed in the coal and lime works, who being distant from any parish church can have no opportunity of attending Divine Service, and therefore spend the Sabbath in idleness and debauchery.'

St Mary's Church, which would have served Newfound Well Farm, was dedicated on September 14, 1878. 'On the morning of consecration,' reported the *Shrewsbury Chronicle,* 'it was a pleasant sight to see the path of the wide common, and fields and lanes, lightened up here and there with the holiday dresses of the labouring classes, as they were wending their way to witness or take part in the ceremony: so strange and yet so grateful this once secluded district.'

Despite Newfound Well Farm's remote situation, it was still part of the territory for the local landed gentry. In 1910 a hunt coursed across the common, chasing a fox over the hilltops. Their quarry evaded them for some nine miles, but, 'at Gate-Hange Well ... Mr Milbank hit him off left-handed through the Rabbit House Covert onto the Silvington Gorse, and from there on through Cleeton Vallets to the Titterstone Hill. He ran over the Hill to the Magpie Covert.'

The chase finished at Newfound Well, 'where they killed him (and "he" proved to be an old vixen) at 3.30pm.' 'This was,' said the correspondent for the *Tenbury Wells Advertiser,* 'a great triumph for our Master, Huntsman and dog pack. No pack of hounds in the kingdom could have stuck to their hunted fox better and with greater determination, in spite of all difficulties, scent at no time being better than what one may describe as a "good holding one".'

The local hunt hammered across the fields around our house.

I could hear their horn and thunder from the house. I hated it. Once, their pursuit led them through the fields below the turkey hatchery. We were outside playing when they came. Red coats and hounds and horses poured across the pasture below Caynham Court. The riders in their scarlet pinks, the whippers-in – for whom our own parliamentary whips are named – cajoling the hounds in their pairs as they all streamed down into the fields, hollering. They looked as if they had rent a crack in the meadow and filled it with a red and brown pyroclastic flow that split the country in two as it churned.

I knew even at that age that such an utter excess of force was not being deployed for efficiency, but for dominance. This was rough music to subdue and silence other humans, a rural power play, a pissing contest, frothing through the green field like the soapy foam at the bottom of a butcher's sink.

The Millichamp family appear to have lived on the farm for most of the nineteenth century. Timothy, born in around 1806, and his family were definitely here by the 1861 census, but likely before, setting up the baths and spring as an enterprise, raising sheep and growing trees.

By 1911 William and Alice Turner and their children lived at Newfound Well. They rented out rooms to Albert Bytheway, his wife Amelia and their sons William and Stanley. Albert, born to Edward and Eliza, was the youngest of six children, the others being John, Emma, Sarah, Lucy and Martha. John and Emma were some ten years senior to the younger children. I suspect John may have died, aged thirteen, in nearby Neen Savage in 1868, meaning that it is unlikely that any of the siblings other than Emma would have known him.

By 1881 Emma had moved out and the remaining children grew up with another child, one-year-old Edward. Although only two years Albert's junior, it is likely that Edward was their nephew, born almost certainly to Emma, apparently out of wedlock, when she was twenty-two.

Thirty years later, Albert and Amelia were living on the Newfound Well Farm, renting rooms in what is now rubble behind me. Sarah, Lucy and Martha were all married to local men and remained nearby. Emma had disappeared. Edward was living with his widowed grandmother Eliza and his three-year-old son, Richard. Edward, by now a quarryman, was a widower at thirty years of age, his wife Elizabeth having died in May 1910. They had been married two and a half years. She was interred at St Paul's parish church in Knowbury.

In his memoir, Alf Jenkins writes about someone whom I think might be the same Edward Bytheway. He was, reports Jenkins, 'often paralysed with cider and on one occasion when he was oblivious to his surroundings, his gang dug him a grave, turfed it around and placed him in it and erected a headstone. When Teddy recovered, he was understandably bewildered to find himself in a grave. He stood up and read this epitaph on the stone, "Here lies a man, and who do you think, old Teddy Bydi, give him more drink. A drink for a dead man for... for when he was alive he was always dry."'

I think about this history, and wonder what I'm hoping to find, sat here on a clammy day on Titterstone Clee, thinking myself a conduit of ghosts.

My attention drifts.

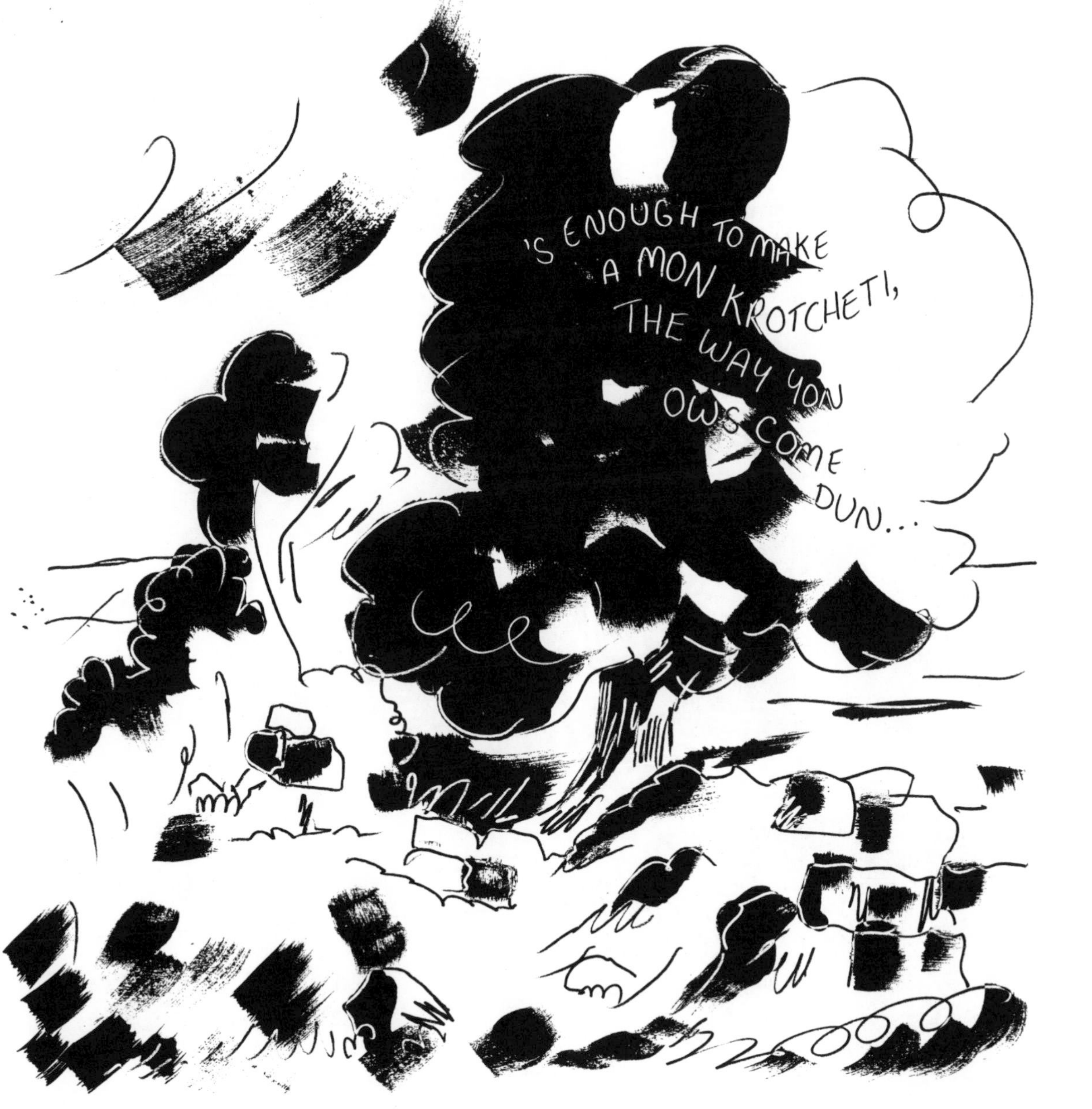
'S ENOUGH TO MAKE A MON KROTCHETI, THE WAY YOU OWS COME DUN...

...ITS SPIR'T SPRAWLIN'
SHITTEN ON THE SIDLUNT
WITH YON SHIP IN THE
GORSTI

It's very early in the morning, it's very cold, and I'm standing one storey up on a shopfront somewhere in Hackney. Inside, in his flat, my best friend is sleeping, and so is Charlie, a Dalmatian-greyhound cross, ginger and white, whom I had left asleep on the living room floor, eyes open but with muzzle to tail, ears twitching, while I climbed out of the window.

I take a drag of my cigarette. At this point in my life, I'm not doing so well. It's a red-eyed, fuck-you kind of not-doing-so-well, dressed up as hey-I'm-just-having-fun-it's-OK kind of not-doing-so-well. I'm not really OK. I'm eating badly, sleeping barely, spending all of my time, money and sanity in the pub and – somewhere amongst all of this – I'm trying to start again. Standing on a roof in Hackney seems to be in perfect keeping with this behaviour.

Below, Mare Street is houndstoothed with taxis, alternately arriving and departing, turning drunk and made-up people out onto the pavement in clouds of artificial scents, taking drunker people away, honking all the while. The traffic lights regulating the junction with Well Street flick red, amber, green, amber, red. Some traffic moves, some doesn't.

Inside the flat there's a table strewn with debris: empty wine glasses, a half-empty bottle of wine, a set of keys, some fast-food flyers picked up from the mat behind the front door, cigarette papers, filters and a packet of Golden Virginia tobacco, the contents of which are at that frustrating point where they turn from moist to brittle ('Put a slice of orange in there!' a friend once told me, 'it'll never dry out'). My laptop is there, too, because I've been talking to a cartoonist friend in Denver about heartbreak. I have also left footprints all over the windowsill.

Outside, I wave at the drunk people in the street below, who are queuing to get into the pub next door. Some wave back, some don't.

Smoking roll-ups up here makes me dig out with sozzled nostalgia a family yarn about Dad. The story goes that one night in his late teens he went on a blind date with a young woman. The affair was derailed before it even began – or so it seemed – by his refusal to share his tobacco, opting instead to sit monosyllabically in a corner all night, dressed in his long coat, squeaking out cigarettes for himself on a little rolling machine. Yet, by some miracle of teenage faith, they became friends, and eventually fell in love, married, and a few years later along came two sons; the young woman in question was my mum, and the sons were Tim and me.

It'll be a couple more months before I realise I'm on a slippery slope to being buried alive, like old Teddy Bydi, and start trying to get my act together. I'll meet Ali, and a new chapter will start. In three years' time, my Dad will be gone, my family left tiny and distorted. Ali and I will marry in a quiet town in the Peak District, and slowly, slowly, life will become new, while my family works itself into its new shape.

But for now, here I am, just an idiot drunk, on a roof in London, working out what the fuck to do next.

Magic

Making my way out of the Newfound Well ruins I find a small piece of pitch-uck. It's about the size of a fifty-pence piece and almost equilaterally pentagonal. It is made of coarse china with a cracked white glaze, and dirty edges.

I thank the mole who turned it out of the ground for me, and resume my walk, rubbing its smooth faces between my fingers in my pocket, where it sits with the piece of coal I picked up twenty minutes earlier, two new talismans to ward off evil, or bring me luck, or show me the way in the dark.

I've always been partial to such things. When I was ten I stripped a sapling to make a wand, whittling the bark away, painting the wood with stain pilfered from the garage, then tying to it rosemary stems and tide-softened glass fragments, bought in little glass bottles from seaside arcades. I'd take it tramping through the rivers with my friend Mark, finding waterfalls, summoning spirits.

Dad made magic important to me. I don't mean magic like pulling a rabbit out of a hat – I've never really been moved by that. It's more the fact that there are still rabbits and hats, despite the overwhelming odds that suggested we should all have been eaten centuries ago, before we even got around to inventing milliners, dress shirts, tuxedos and stages.

Magic is joyous nonsense. Absurdity and profundity rolled into one. It is the contradictory, the paradoxical, two truths at once held in imperfect, impossible equilibrium. These breathe in and out with the sense of the possibility they hold, the mystical something that bridges the gap between tedium and astonishment.

Magic is the gaps between memories, where stories – fallible, imaginative, confabulatory – take root. In so doing, magic becomes myth.

One such myth, twenty-five years burnished, floats to the surface. I was about ten years old, walking home from the village school. I had turned off the main road and was walking down the little road to our house when a ball of light, burning white, a little larger than a honeydew melon – a fruit we'd eat slices of at home covered in soft brown sugar and whose form I knew well – appeared from behind me, moving at velocity, and causing me to stumble from the curbstones on which I was balanced. The fireball made no noise, gave off no heat. It sailed past me at shoulder height, before vanishing somewhere ahead of me.

'In many parts of Britain,' Hole tells us, 'and especially in Wales, belief in the Corpse-Candle was once very common. This was a small flame, or ball of fire, which was seen floating from the churchyard towards the house of a dying person, or one who, though still in health, was destined to die shortly. It travelled always by the same route as the funeral would subsequently take. A small blue flame denoted the death of a child, a larger and yellowish one, that of an adult.'

I saw that fireball twenty-five years ago, and I still remember it, plain as day, even though I am equally sure that the event in question never even happened.

Another myth. I'm with my friend Laurence and his younger sister, Imogen, out behind their house, looking south. We are stood stock-still. The meadow is shimmering. I see its wetness. Yellow flowers are studded in it. A lilac haze, like petrol on water, hangs hay-fever-fumed above. The countryside, trees are in front, swaying; fractal leaves, movement in movements in movements, waving. I see the brook running true, hear it, see its wetness, too. Birds sing, grasses click; fly-buzz heard, distant farm noises, and the sky is a cornflower petal one million times its natural size.

For years, I had situated this vision of spring fecundity as having been experienced from the western edge of St Mary's graveyard, looking north, with Caynham Camp's mass looming above the willows, and not in the rectory fields opposite. A strange, anomalous, technicolour memory divorced from any biographical anchor – why was I there? Did it even happen?

It feels like a small thing, but it took me twenty years to realise my mistake. It was one day, six years ago. I had driven the ninety-odd miles north from Bristol in search of the meadow. I arrived in Caynham in a spit of rain, parked next to the garages near the turkey-hatchery offices, then walked up towards the main road. It was April, but the weather was still more winter than spring. I was here trying to take a break from the slip-slide into imminent heartbreak. I was twenty-nine.

I climbed the stile into a field that was at one point called Brick Kiln Piece and headed east, cutting across an adjacent cow pasture to the fields behind the church. I arrived at where I thought I had been all those years ago, but upon ending my pilgrimage I realised there was no river there: just mud, ploughed soil, the church boundary, and the slope up to the hill fort.

I felt all at once at home and left behind. I sat down on the grass at the field's edge and stared at the red clay on my boots. What now? I sniffed the air, and have you ever smelled how the air smells when sheep are near? Lanolin, like grass and sunshine and dung and citrus and hay and husbandry, which makes the air feel like you've put your tongue on a battery? And there it was – magic, both *heimat* and *unheimlich*, both homely and uncanny.

I try and try to hold on to that sensation as the years oxidise around me, both there and not there, both farmhouse and ruin, both nostalgia-seared postcard and cold despondent realisation of a truth, stuck with the simultaneity of its objective reality and its patina of memory-rust, a new layer with every recollection, distorting it; a drinks can in Benson's Brook becoming a discarded mediaeval chalice.

I returned to the road to look at what was left of the old village school. I knew it had closed, and – because Google exists and because I was curious and because I had been thinking about this a lot – I had found out that the playground where I avoided playing football but still managed to catch one in the face was now a piss-poor excuse for someone's new garden, that the creaky corrugated plastic veranda, mossy and perished, the temporary classrooms, the toilet block, with its mural of jungle animals, were all gone, and that the main hall, barely the size of a double-car garage, was now someone's home.

In my unfocused arbitrary melancholy I raged at the loss of that place, of a building, a function. Is this how the horrific pledge to 'the good old days' is made? To plant my flag, while ignoring the irony of having grown up five hundred feet away, in a house built upon layers and layers of other people's memories, angry that someone else was now doing the same to me?

I think about the school toilet block now, those bright, bold giraffes and snakes, and remember how it was inside that unheated breeze-block building, pissing in the winter, that I first learned that our insides were hot, watching steam rise from our urine and giggling.

I think about our school field – now overgrown and under consideration for redevelopment – its forgotten sandbox filled with dog and fox turds, the leylandii at the rear of the semi-detached houses which backed on to the playing field and faced the road on which the school sat and which was the same road where Sammy the cat got run over (Mum, Tim and I hugging in the lounge, crying).

I remember the sheep incursions, the tree where Mark and Shaun sat and I felt left out. I remember the big ice-cream-carton time capsule we buried as a class in 1993. What memories went into that brittle oblong? Probably something about Liverpool FC, probably a VHS, an episode of *Neighbours* (didn't watch until 1997), an episode of *Eastenders* (watched that between 2003 and 2004) or *Coronation Street* (2005–2013) or a cartoon. What books (pre-Harry Potter)? A newspaper? The *Ludlow Advertiser*?

I want to dig it up. I want to dig it up before the builders do, and throw its contents everywhere, its expiring plastic and stinking paper leftovers, its rotten innards. It is a broken heart, a lie, a mess, a waste. Who else even remembers it? What's the fucking point? Kids putting shit in a box and burying it under the earth, no gravestone, as if we'll remember the dead cassettes and copies of *Smash Hits*, the crippled wrinkle of video tape? I want to do an exhumation, just like this, selfish and bitter, staring down the detritus of our febrile imaginations, pathetic and unwanted; the caravan my brother doesn't remember, the time capsule I no longer know anyone to ask about, a forgotten farmhouse, a pile of rocks, a piece of crockery.

I'm angry not because the places are gone, but because I'm scared of that magic leaving. I want to hold on to that feeling, whatever that feeling is: comfort, safety, joy, the ache of an old building, the smell of a mouldy caravan, nine years old and understanding for the first time the tacit transience of stuff, seeing that whole little wheeled house transmute into different states, different substances, all while looking for an adventurer's treasure, thinking these things will be around forever, but only just starting to learn that they will not.

The Three Forked Pole

I walk south from Newfound Well, following the northern and western edges of the field system of Random Farm, passing a duck pond which looks pale in the light. I think about fish and ducks twitching around in that pool of rock-dust soup. I climb a bit towards the slight horizon of Hoar's Edge which in turn gives way in a little dip. Then the sun comes out and the wind picks up, and there it is. I take a little gasp in excitement.

The Three Forked Pole stands right in front of me. It is a tree trunk, tall and straight, sunk into the Clee soil and stripped bare of all branches, except the base of two short boughs, which conspire with the remains of the trunk to form a sort of trident. The whole thing looks like something kinder than a claw, but still claw-like.

A pole is the most prominent feature on a map of 1571, notes to which read: 'a fforked pole near to a place where an old Stone Crosse stood formerly'. It's marked on an estate map of 1769, too. A nineteenth-century newspaper article notes a Thomas By-the-Way as being 'keeper of the Cross at the top of Titterstone Clee Hill', and it is mentioned again in a newspaper article in 1928.

Nowadays, the pole marks roughly where three parishes – Hopton Wafers, Cleeton St Mary and Doddington – meet. Before the parish boundaries were redrawn, however, it stood at the intersection of the ancient parishes of Coreley, Earl's Ditton, Hopton, the Catherton township and the Chapelry of Farlow.

Looking south, from the pole you can see the bump of Trout Pit, which was allowed to drown in 1922 after extraction became too expensive, and Barn Pit next door which closed around the time of the General Strike in 1926. Those were the last pits to extract coal on Titterstone.

Major quarrying also began to slow down around the same time, with the closure of the Dhustone Quarry. Titterstone Quarry closed in the late 1950s, and the Incline Quarry followed suit in the 1960s.

Towards the end of 1969, tests began in the wastes of the common land to see if there were still viable coal seams. Talk of open-cast mining soon caught the attention of the hill communities, and local opposition quickly rose to the stripping of the thin soils, to the enclosure of common land, to the destruction of fragile ecosystems, to interference with the water table, to the dust and dirt and pollution.

Mr Cyrill Yapp, Chairman of the Clee Hill Commoners' Association voiced his concerns to the *Birmingham Daily Post* in November 1969, as did other members of the community – farmers, incomers, visitors alike.

'The firm has not jumped any guns,' Mr Basil Poole, a mining consultant engaged in the proposals is quoted as saying in response. 'It has let the planning authority know and it is in negotiation with the authority over the whole question of working in this area. Planning permission will have to be obtained before actual mining can begin.'

A. J. Rees, writing three years later in the same newspaper, records that by the summer of 1972 the Three-Forked Pole 'had lost its three branches, and the shaft, snapped at the base, lay in prone decay among grass and rushes, having succumbed at last to years ... of Titterstone's weather.'

He goes on to report that on July 8 of that year, the Clee Hill Commoners' Association erected, 'a new pole, an oak tree with three natural branches, specially selected from a Bridgnorth estate. Spotting its twenty-foot outline across the moor, even in poor visibility,' he continues, 'should be a little easier than seeking its predecessor's remains among the undergrowth.'

This new pole Rees describes probably replaced one erected in the 1920s by the Price family, after the preceding pole had fallen in a storm.

The Three Forked Pole

This is situated near the site of the old Watsall Pit and near Random Farm. It has been a land mark for many hundreds of years and stands where three parishes and three estates meet. This photograph shows the Price family having just re-erected a new pole in the 1920s.

These poles are more than just way-finding devices. They are a symbol of both change and stasis, permanence and impermanence, but most importantly, of the people who have lived and worked here for so long. They are a symbol of the commons, as A. J. Rees concludes: 'threatened first by commercial exploitation for coal and clay – and this threat still lurks ominously in the background – the commons are now in dispute over registration, and the Commoners' Association will welcome any evidence, particularly documentary, to prove that these lands have been common from time immemorial.'

In response to both public pressure and 'commercial considerations', the strip-mining plans were scaled back drastically. 'It was reluctantly accepted,' wrote L. A. Crump and R. Donnelly in *Opencast coal mining: a unique opportunity for Clee Hill Quarry*, 'that future development of Clee Hill Quarry would take place between Dhustone and Incline Quarries with removal of substantial volumes of Coal Measures overburden an integral part of future quarrying.'

Exploratory work began again on the hill in the 1980s. Planning Permission was awarded in August 1988, and between October 1988 and July 1992, the workings extracted 322,000 tonnes of saleable coal from 2.5×106 m^3 of overburden from the Clee Hill Quarry site. The work was constrained to thirty-three hectares of land between the Dhustone and Incline faces. The new quarry, visible from Hoar's Edge, has permission to take its operations all the way to 2048.

I put my ear to the old grey wood. I feel the pole vibrate and shudder in the wind. I can hear it moving like a sigh as the wind wraps around the bark. It hums with energy, with life, dead as it is. As it moves, the wood knocks gently but with an implacable force against the arms of my glasses. I wrap my own arms around the pole, holding it tighter, pressing my cheek flesh against the grey grooves, beard hair caught in the bark's valleys, tugging, moving, at one. My arms ache, but still I hold on, its residual warmth from the September sun matching my own.

After some time, I step back, suddenly a bit embarrassed.

The pole looks down at me and smiles.

Ghosts

I turn around and walk back towards the summit. As I make my way across the heathland the radar station comes into view. It is a squat one-storey concrete building, from which large masts grow up like trees. All around, concrete stanchions hold up old chain-link fences, topped by barbed wire.

I'm taking roughly the same route across the hill that was used during a celebration called the Titterstone Wake. Burne reports that the Wake was held on the last Sunday in August to celebrate the harvest. The hill communities would meet at the Three Forked Pole, from which the unmarried men and women would process together along 'Tea-Kettle Alley', a makeshift stone-lined holloway, at the end of which the older and married women could be found making tea with water from the nearby Shirley Brook, and distributing watercress to the procession as it passed by.

Titterstone resident Richard Jones recalled that everyone dressed in their best clothes. The women, he recalled, were 'fine stand-up handsome wenches ... well-dressed too, nothing like'em now; but ye wouldna know 'em the next day with a bag of coal strapped on their backs.'

Jones said everyone would then meet at the summit and 'the games began – kiss in the ring, racing and jumping for hats or shoes or neckties, wrestling, boxing and so forth: to the inevitable accompaniment of beer sold on the hill. Often no work was done that week, but the whole time till Saturday night was spent in keeping up the wake.'

Jones attended the Wake many times up until 1846, at which point he said the tradition was 'fast declining'. Thomas Powell, however, recalled that as late as 1861 the tradition was still surviving. He also said that the men and boys took it in turns to sit in the Giant's Chair, a pile of rocks at the summit, and sing rhymes, before walking to the Pole to meet the women.

As I get closer to the radar station, I can see a security light blinking on-off-on-off on the near side of the building, seemingly at will. Dad's friend and colleague Phil told me erratic alarms and lights weren't uncommon. He recounted to me recently the story of how he was once called out at three in the morning to attend to an intruder alarm at the radar station.

'I arrived halfway up the hill,' he told me, 'to be met by the largest number of police I had ever seen, some carrying machine guns, handguns, police dogs and the big search lights that nearly blinded me as I approached.

'The wind at the top can be unpredictable in its strength and direction,' explains Phil. 'On this occasion it had activated a single knock alarm on the AR5 Radar's garage doors. I confirmed the alarm was erroneous and caused by the wind.

'As I reset the alarm I failed to notice that the police had cleared not only the building but the hill in its entirety and that I no longer had the benefit of their lovely bright torches. I became aware of something rubbing the back of my leg and froze in fear only to discover that a sheep was using my leg as something to scratch itself on. I swear to God I left the hill a lot faster than I arrived.'

A sensation of the uncanny wasn't uncommon on the hill. Dad told me that one morning, two of his colleagues were returning from inspecting one of the radars in heavy snow, when they spotted footprints leading towards the top of a quarry face. The engineers followed the footsteps and saw they continued over the cliff, without returning. They called the emergency services and carried out an extensive search, but no evidence could be found that anyone had fallen. Nonplussed, the engineers returned to the station, and their experience became a ghost story.

There were other stories, too, like the one about the engineer who spent a night alone at the station, plagued by footsteps echoing around the long trunk corridor. He told my Dad how the steps had stalled outside his room, lingering before resuming their ambulation and petering out into nothingness. His dog cowered in the corner. He peered into the hallway. Nobody was there. The engineer, an old military man, refused to ever spend the night in the station again.

I've never seen a ghost. Our only shared family ghost story revolves around a family walk around the outside of Ludlow Castle, one midsummer. Tim and I were excited because we had learned about the story of the ghost of Marian de la Bruyere. Her story came from a factually questionable fourteenth-century romance called *Fouke le Fitz Waryn*.

In the eleventh century, Gilbert de Lacy, a local lord, had become involved in a dispute with nobleman Josce de Dinan over the latter's occupancy of nearby Ludlow Castle. One night while de Dinan was abroad, a lady in his retinue named Marian de la Bruyere had feigned illness in order to stay at the castle, so she could meet her lover, a de Lacy soldier named Arnold de Lisle whose escape from the castle she had previously facilitated.

That evening, de la Bruyere let a leather ladder down from her window, allowing de Lisle to climb up to her chambers. However, he had brought with him a force of one hundred men; they followed him up the ladder, and overran the castle. Gilbert de Lacy gained Ludlow Castle, but not before de la Bruyere had killed her lover with his own sword for his treachery, and thrown herself from the castle walls in remorse.

Apparently, tonight was the one night of the year that her ghost came to visit, a flash of white, a ghostly scream from that tower, at whose base a yew tree now grew.

What I didn't know, but my parents did, is that at that moment there was an open-air Shakespeare performance happening in the castle walls, so when a great big scream suddenly sounded, they didn't bat an eyelid. I, however, jumped high in the air and ran, startled. Dad laughed, and I fell over and hit the gravelly path, skinned my knee, and then yelled at Dad, telling him it was his fault that I tripped up.

He simply laughed again and said, 'It wasn't me, it was the ghost!'

I huff and puff up the slope past the station, to where the peak of the hill begins to flatten out and you can see all the radars. It's not the steepest bit of the hill, but steep enough for someone like me whose fitness has always – thanks to a combination of distraction and disinclination – been on the wrong side of average.

While catching my breath, I look at the radars. They sprout above the surface of the hill like little puffballs, just as they did when I was little. They are visible from all around, despite early promises made to the Shropshire branch of the Council for the Preservation of Rural England in 1961 that, 'all that would be seen from the Ludlow side was a slim one-hundred-foot aerial. The buildings of the station would be hidden from view and would be below the skyline.'

When we lived here, the local Gateway's supermarket freezer aisle, or the till at the newsagent, were the site for any number of whispered conspiracies about their purpose: the CIA, MI5, the military, aliens.

One day, Dad took Tim and me up a ladder and inside one of the radomes, the big domes that sat over the radars themselves. The radome was being serviced, and there were men, high up on ladders, taking panels in and out. This let the October brightness in now and then and when it broke through the gaps it looked like fish were turning on the ceiling. It was like a geodesic cathedral, with those big translucent triangular panels that looked like they were made from glazed eggshell, or a biosphere for warm air and invisible information, science and space re-ordered, a profane orb, as mystical to me as a crystal ball.

I haven't set foot in the station in well over twenty-five years, but that place, those people, the smell of valves, the squeaky floors, the scent of cleaners' bleach, the echoing corridor, the smell of tea and cigarettes, the green glow of the radar screen – these were my earliest memories of adult work, and will forever be my image of whatever it was that Dad did.

```
07-MAR-87 10:13:24 COMMS      PC 006550    *       LINK
07-MAR-87 10:15:09 COMMS      PC 006550    *       LINK
07-MAR-87 10:17:08 COMMS      PC 006550    *       LINK
07-MAR-87 10:35:11 COMMS      PC 006550    *       LINK
07-MAR-87 10:35:16 COMMS      PC 006550    *       LINK K
07-MAR-87 10:35:46 COMMS      PC 006550    *       LINK K
07-MAR-87 10:35:57 COMMS      PC 006550    *       LINK KM
07-MAR-87 10:41:11 COMMS      PC 006550    *       LINK KM
07-MAR-87 10:41:22 COMMS      PC 006550    *       LINK KMO
07-MAR-87 10:43:11 COMMS      PC 006550    *       LINK KMO
07-MAR-87 10:48:11 COMMS      PC 006550    *       LINK KMO
07-MAR-87 10:53:12 COMMS      PC 006550    *       LINK KMO
07-MAR-87 10:53:27 COMMS      PC 006550    *       LINK KMO
07-MAR-87 10:53:57 COMMS      PC 006550    *       LINK KMO
07-MAR-87 10:54:18 COMMS      PC 006550    *       LINK KMO
07-MAR-87 10:56:13 COMMS      PC 006550    *       LINK KMO
07-MAR-87 10:56:39 COMMS      PC 006550            LINK
07-MAR-87 10:57:08 COMMS      PC 006550            LIN
07-MAR-87 10:57:13 COMMS      PC 00
07-MAR-87 11:03:16 COMMS      PC
07-MAR-87 11:03:20 COMMS
07-MAR-87 11:06:18 COM
07-MAR-87 11:07:59 COM
07-MAR-87 11:15
07-MAR-87 11
```

2 CONNECTED TO LATCC

1 CONNECTED TO CAMU 1

System run down to robo DCO after log examination on DC1.

TOO MANY HARDWARE ERRORS

INITIALISED, ABORTED UNACKNOWLEDGED FRAMES
NNECTED TO LATCC
INITIALISED, TOO MANY HARDWARE ERRORS
NECTED TO LATCC
INITIALISED, TOO MANY HARDWARE ERRORS
NECTED TO LATCC
INITIALISED, TOO MANY HARDWARE ERRORS
ECTED TO LATCC
NITIALISED, TOO MANY HARDWARE ERRORS
ECTED TO LATCC
NITIALISED HARDWARE ERRORS
CTED TO
NITIAL DWARE ERRORS
TS ARE ERRORS
50 E ERRORS

0150 RRORS
0166 RORS
ced nothing

For me, the place remains a living breathing thing, its cathodes and resistors and domes burning gently in the night, making quiet maps, and sharing them with the station's ghosts.

Moving towards the peak, I see a distant curl of smoke to the north, towards Church Stretton.

In the final weeks of 1922 and into the New Year, *The Belfast Telegraph* tells us that sixteen miles from Titterstone the county of Shropshire, 'was being gradually consumed by a mystery fire.

'Two miles out of Shrewsbury rising columns of smoke are bursting through the surface of farmland. They come from some underground conflagration, the origin of which no-one can explain. The earth is burning and the fire is slowly eating its mysterious way along an ever-increasing area, to the complete bewilderment of the county and to the dreadful joy of those who champion the old-fashioned idea of eternal punishment.

'Scores of barrels of water have been carried to the spot. Coughing and spluttering farm labourers empty them on the roasting fires, and the only result is a hissing cloud of mingled mist and steam. Trenches have been dug in an attempt to isolate the burning part of Shropshire, but the mystery just assumes more intensity and eats its way underneath them. Men have dug six feet down and still fail to reach the real fire. The earth, however, is so intensely hot that a stick pushed two or three feet below the surface soon chars.'

As I write this, the wildfires in California have consumed nearly two million acres of countryside and dozens of communities, including the town of Paradise; thousands of lives have been disrupted, and over one hundred people killed.

One day in San Francisco, my brother said, it was as dark as fog with the drifting smoke, and I imagine ash settling like snowflakes on his son's shoulders.

I watches the skies
I watches the animals
the things I've watched
for many years...
guides to tell
us the weather

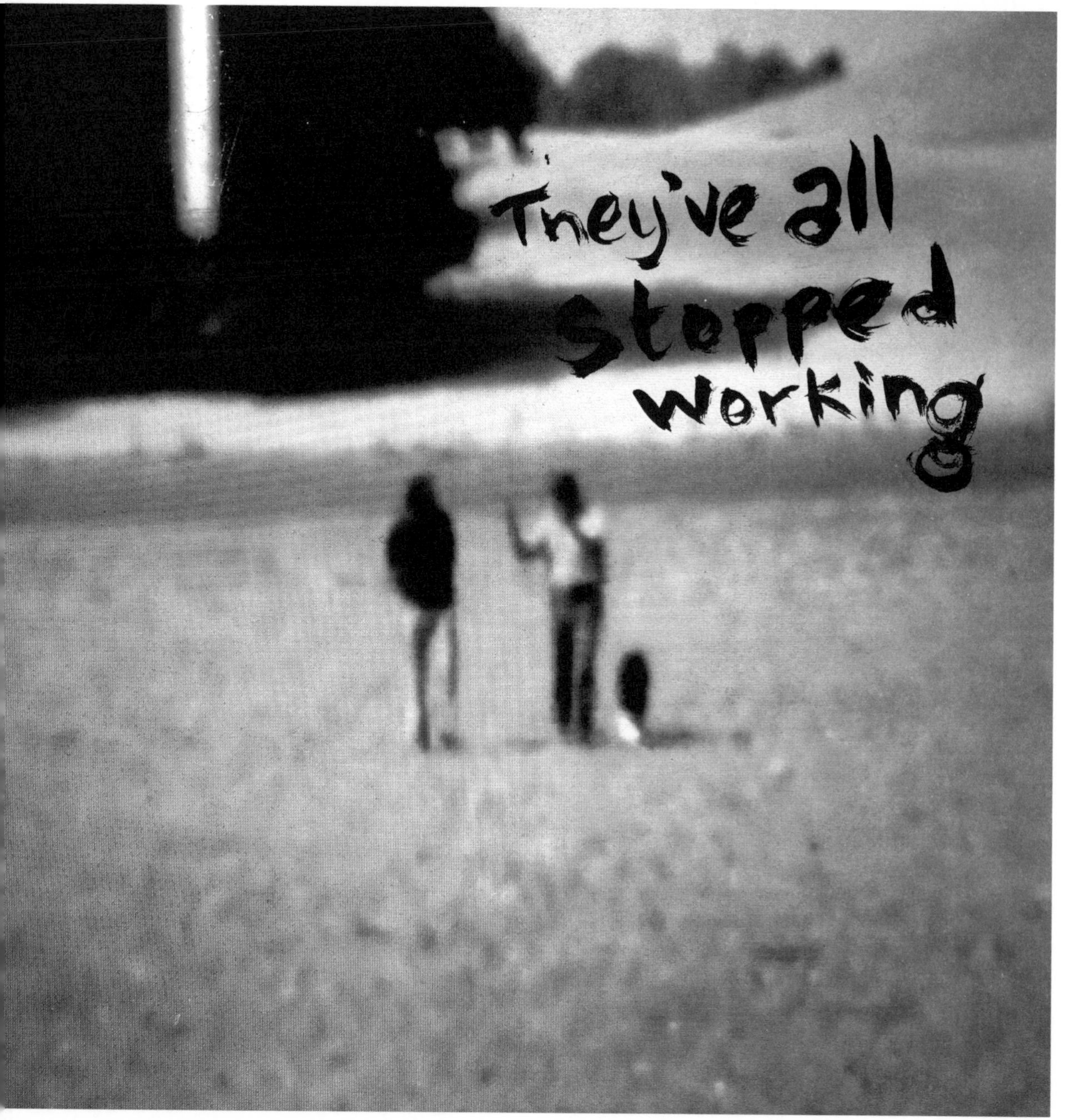
They've all
stopped
working

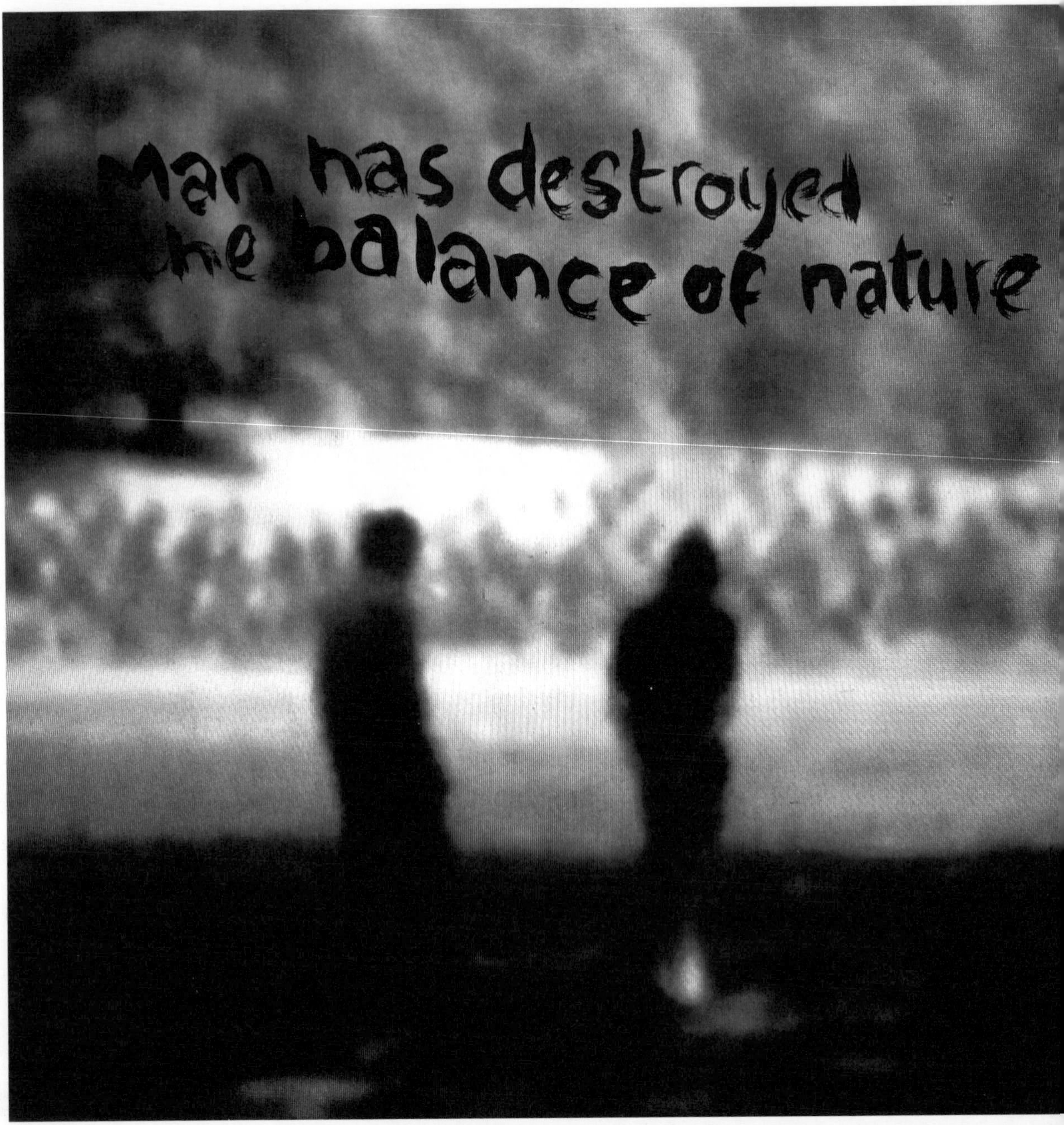
man has destroyed
the balance of nature

it was built most
perfect and we've
disturbed it

Ten
The flower
fadeth

Prognosis

Dad fell ill two days after Tim boarded his flight back to America. Mum called the paramedics on Sunday night, and by Monday Dad was back in hospital.

More tests followed and the new week stretched out like a rheumatic limb. We all became more tightly wound, with the feeling of having drunk too much coffee, only all of the time stuffed full of sadness and fear, but still playing the part of positivity and practicality – because what else was there to do?

Mum rang me on Wednesday night. We were in Bristol.

'We have some news,' she said. 'Could you come and see us?'

We drove straight to the hospital the next morning, the M5 sludging around outside the car for the hundredth time.

We arrive and make our way to Dad's ward. We say our hellos and sit at Dad's bedside, waiting for the family room to become available. Without privacy, it's clear my parents don't want to tell us the news, and the exertion of making idle chat feels acute, like peeling my fingertips from the surface of an ice cube.

After a while, the small talk fades and a nurse beckons us over.

We enter the family room. It is very hot. Children's toys, a blank TV screen, half a dozen DVDs sit in a corner. A window looks out into a small garden. Wooden chairs, the bottoms of all their legs scuffed. By what? Vacuum? People's feet? Bleachy mops?

Mum and Dad sit opposite us.

Tim is still in San Francisco.

Dad starts sentences and Mum finishes them.

The cancer is untreatable.

We drive home, dazed. Two days later, Mum calls me again.

On Sunday, I drive back to Devon and go straight to the hospital; Tim is in California, Ali is at home in Bristol with a cold.

I walk into the ward. Mum is already there, speaking with the nurses at the reception desk as the night shift hands over to the day shift. I carry on through the double doors opposite the nurses' station.

Dad is in his bed, sitting up, gaping for air. His eyes are glassy. He looks almost amphibious for a horrible moment. I feel guilty saying that, but it's true; bodies are made stranger by illness. His eyes catch mine. He ranges around slightly, like washing in the breeze. He's gently absent and for a moment he is all function, all form. Where is Dad? Then he catches sight of me, and smiles and a trapdoor opens beneath me.

I kiss him on his forehead, and ask him how his night was, and while he's replying, I text my brother: 'here with mum and dad please call as soon as you get this.'

Tim has barely been back in San Francisco a week, so I know he'll be reluctant to get on another plane. Not for any selfish reason, and not because it involves leaving his young son and his wife again, though I know he doesn't want to do that, but because to come back will be to face something we aren't ready to face, and to accept the risk he could be in a plane watching a shit film or at Heathrow waiting for his baggage or in a WH Smith's buying a magazine he won't read or on a train somewhere between here and there, when it happens.

We thought we had more time, but we don't; it is already happening, and there's nothing that I can do to stop it.

Just looking into flights...
will call shortly

Ok great. There about to
move Dad into a side room
so that will help x

You holding up ok?

Caynham Court.

HIS substantial mansion, the seat of Sir William Michael Curtis, Bart., is situate about two and three quarter miles south-east of Ludlow. It occupies a commanding position and the grounds afford great diversity of picturesque scenery, fern-clad dells and leafy glades meeting one at almost every turn. Many fine trees adorn the landscape, conspicuous among these being some magnificent cedars, beeches, and poplars near the house. Immediately in front of the mansion is a piece of rising ground, known as the Catholic Hill, near which are the beagle kennels and the keeper's cottage; from this site a very pretty view of Caynham Court is obtained. The estate was formerly a possession of the Calcott family, from whom it was purchased in 1852 by the late Sir William Curtis, who renovated the interior of the house, and made some additions to it. Prior to possession by the Calcotts, the place seems to have belonged to the Oldham family, for in 1789 we find Joseph Oldham, of Caynham Court, Sheriff of Shropshire. The large entrance hall is adorned with hunting trophies and many good pictures : among the latter is a full length portrait of the first baronet, by Sir Thomas Lawrence, and another striking picture is a portrait group of the uncles of the late Sir William. From this square hall the principal staircase ascends ; its walls are also well-lined with pictures, and the various corridors are likewise adorned with many unframed canvases.

The dining room is spacious, and well-lighted by a large bay window of three lights, which extends across one end ; this commands a charming view across the park, right opposite being a magnificent cedar, which adds to the beauty of the landscape. The walls of this apartment are of a red tone, and the white ceiling has a moulded cornice ; the doors are of polished maple. Eleven pictures adorn the walls ; conspicuous over the marble mantel-piece is a fine portrait, by Sir Thomas Lawrence, of George IV., among whose personal friends the second Sir William Curtis was included. A portrait of the father of the first baronet, by Chamberlayne, also hangs here, and a portrait of the present dowager Lady Curtis is by Phillips. Another work by Chamberlayne is a portrait of Miss Betty Lamb. The third Sir William was himself an artist of considerable repute, and his skill is shown by many fine landscapes which adorn the walls of Caynham Court—two note-worthy examples hang in the dining room, the one being a view in the park of Netheravon, in Wiltshire, the residence of Sir Michael Hicks-Beach, to whom the dowager Lady Curtis is related. On a table near the window is a fine polished oak coffer, made from timber cut down in the year of the present baronet's birth and presented to him on attaining his majority. An oak sideboard of similar character stands in a recess between two doorways at the end of the room; two columns, with moulded bases and capitals, rise to the ceiling on either side.

The drawing room is another fine apartment; its ceiling is decorated in white and gold, and numerous pictures hang on the walls. The panels of the window frames are delicately painted with pretty landscapes the work of the Sir William Curtis previously mentioned. The smoking room is a cosy apartment which commands a good view; its walls are nearly covered with pictures, many of which appropriately indicate the favourite pastimes of their owner. These include various water-colour hunting sketches of a humorous character, and oil paintings of hounds and horses. There are also one or two good oil landscapes, and on either side of the fireplace are well-filled book-cases; and above the mirror are four trophies of sport by flood and field in the shape of otters and fox

Between the dining and drawing rooms is the library, which, before the alterations made by the late Sir William Curtis, was the entrance hall; this is a most comfortable, home-like, and cheerful room, from whose windows a charming view is obtained towards the high Vinnals, and below runs the Ledwych river, a stream famed for good trout fishing.

we sneaked in the cellar it was very dark

then we went
to the room
with all the
books

they weren't real

Eleven
God called me in my younger days

Time

My memory is on the fritz; the building blocks of the day – hours, minutes seconds – have all gone elastic. Time ticks. The chronology becomes confused; motorways, country roads, hospital corridors, empty canteens, bad coffee, tired eyes, holding hands, beta-blockers, remembering, forgetting, emergency emergency emergency, in-patient, out-patient, medical furniture, diagnoses, medicines, prognoses, conversations, scents, sounds, respiration, loose change, parking charges, more roads, more driving, more bad coffee, more driving, more news, more more, always more questions.

It's amazing what a brain besieged will and won't remember, what remarkable feats of endurance it can achieve, and what simple tasks it'll make a right mess of carrying out. I can set fire to my beard on the allotment with a mismanaged leaf incinerator, but I can't remember what happened this morning, two weeks ago, two years ago, was that really in 2012?

One minute I'm here writing this and the next it's September 2016. I am home alone on a Saturday. I am being pestered by the cat. I am trying to put a zine together, but she keeps standing on my laptop, typing things like *fwezwegra* and *sdfgf* with her little paws. I try to put her off by gently placing her on the floor at my feet, where she slinks around the table legs and squeaks and meeps in protest. I think she wants me to play with her or to feed her.

I make to chide her, gently, to encourage her to find her own fun while I finish off a piece of writing. I open my mouth. Other than talking to her throughout the morning, I haven't spoken out loud in thirty-six hours. It is evening now. So I open my mouth and, for some reason, say simply, 'miaow'.

Later, my mum calls and we are talking about Dizzy.

She says, 'You're getting very attached to that cat.'

I say of course I am, she's our little pal, why wouldn't I be attached to her?

'Just be careful,' she says.

Now it's eleven pm the next day and I'm frantic; Dizzy hasn't come in. I can't find her. She won't respond to our calls. I'm in the street with a torch, looking under cars. I'm walking up and down the road; I can't lose her; I have to find her; I have to hold this together; if I can't find her, I can't hold anything together, and I feel terrified because I've spent all year trying to hold myself together, trying to be soft but stoic. I can't lose Dizzy, I can't fail. I can't let us all down. She comes home, oblivious to my panic.

Now it's a month later and I'm walking around Sainsbury's, thinking about things, looking at the shelves. Tins, bags, boxes. I've just been given a new five-pound note by the cashpoint. Outside the air is cold, the sky is black, but the sun is out. I want to drive to work to pick up some paper I had organised to be delivered there, but I can't because people are running a half marathon and the roads are closed. It's autumn now, and I am thinking how life is rich and I am rich with it.

Now it's twilight in Manchester another month later, and Ali, her dad Colin and I are walking down Carrwood, a gross strip of detached houses knocked down and rebuilt as Argos mansions with big gates and weird statues and private security guards sitting outside in CCTV vans, eating sandwiches. It is a few weeks before Colin's cancer diagnosis, and two months before my dad's. We're watching the bats, while the security guards just eat their sandwiches and play on their phones, a dull glow on their faces in the dusk.

Now it's Mum and Ali and me at the Oasis Café, sometime in February the following year, drinking coffee from the self-service machine; Mum is gently brave. She is holding it together. Mum and Ali and me at the Oasis Café, where time is an inert pond, nurses, patients, visitors bobbing like ducks on its surface. We tread water, Mum and Ali and me at the Oasis Café. Plastic chairs, cold chips, one ketchup sachet after another, tin-foil-feeling between incisors as I bite them open in turn, sliding creakily, enamel squeaking. Downstairs in the Yeo ward, Dad eats his dinner in his bed, upstairs, Mum and Ali and me at the Oasis Café, for the last time.

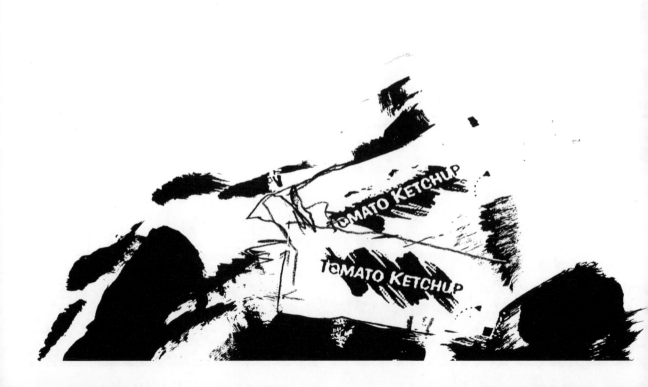

The hospice

My still-jet-lagged brother boards his flight back to the UK and Dad is transferred to a hospice in the hospital grounds. He has his own room. We are thankful for the privacy, only dimly recognising what has happened to make his bed available.

My Dad's sister and nephew begin to drive down from Liverpool, and my parents' oldest friends, our godparents, leave East Anglia and head for Devon.

They arrive the next morning. I pick Tim up from Exeter St David's train station that evening. While waiting for him, I look towards an old Natwest ATM in the station where I once had my debit card cloned when I was twenty years old. I found out when I tried to withdraw cash the next morning and discovered all my money gone. 'What did I do last night?' I thought to myself, before realising what had happened. It turned out to be an expensive takeaway – mild, coconut-sweet vegetable korma, pilau rice, free poppadoms, a prawn jalfrezi – eaten in my house on Bonhay Road, a few dozen yards away from where I'm parked, engine ticking as it cools.

Tim emerges, blinking from the station. He looks tired, but OK. As we drive off, my brain fails me, and I suddenly can't remember the way back to the hospice. I ask Tim to use his mobile phone to get some directions, and he directs the two of us to the wrong hospital. I'm relieved to see him and it's nice to spend that extra time in the car, rattling around a damp, quiet Exeter, even if we are due somewhere else with more urgency.

We make it to the hospice. Everyone but Mum has left and gone to bed.

We get a Pizza Hut pizza and share the leftover slices with the nurses.

Saturday morning I ... came then through
drew back the curtains. I saw a flock of sheep
window I saw a flock of sheep
the front garden. I didn't do much
the rest of the day. On Sunday Morning
went for a walk in Bircher. We
walked past some pheasants bird shelters. Then suddenly
flock of pheasants flew across the
path in front of us. The rest of the
way was woodlands. We went down into
leaves. We picked
a valley filled with roast infront
some chestnuts up to when we went home
of the fire when we passed an
on the way. back with a huge hole
old bridge That evening we had
in the centre. word 'Master Mind'.
it was 'Reet'.
chestnuts.

Croft Castle

Drive out of Caynham, past the old gatehouse of Caynham Court, past Caynham House, where His Excellency Major-General The Honourable Richard Clement Moody retired in 1881, in repose from his colonial work in the Falklands Islands and British Columbia, where he established Port Moody, faced down Ned McGowan in a bloodless war, had two illegitimate children with his housekeeper, and had eleven children by his wife – the inheritors of his £24,000 sum and estates after he died from a stroke in Bournemouth in 1887.

Carry on south, past the site at Ashford Carbonell where the Caynham village school was moved in 2011, over the Teme, over the railway line, along the A49. Take a right at Woofferton, driving past the field of masts, poles and wires, flickering through shrubs and a chain-link fence, that comprise the transmitting station, fingers in a field that lies across a county line, one skyward hand in Shropshire, the other in Herefordshire.

Woofferton was one of a few sites chosen in 1941 by the BBC to establish transmitting stations at the request of the Ministry of Information who wanted more capacity for overseas radio programming with greater broadcasting reach to counteract Nazi propaganda and support the resistance.

Construction began in earnest in 1943. In *Fifty years of transmitting at BBC Woofferton 1943–1993,* Jeff Cant relates how the station was built on 'one-hundred acres of low-lying land which had been a lake in prehistoric times. When the snow melted in April 1943 the site once again became a lake. The riggers and aerial switching assistants had to be provided with fishing waders.'

BY THE WATERS OF TEME

Not only was initiative shown by masters and boys in organizing activities, but also there was plenty of individual initiative shown. I remember when Dick Hazell, with a broken leg in plaster, was unable to bicycle to Moor Park for classes. My application for petrol to take him by car was refused and I had to tell him regretfully that he would have to do his best to work on his own. The next thing I heard was that he had borrowed a horse and trap in the village, and thereafter he drove each day triumphantly to classes. Sometimes initiative was embarrassing. On one occasion Patrick Halsey found a telephone message awaiting him, 'Telephone call from the B.B.C. Wofferton. Apparently some of the boys have been climbing about on this property. They say the name 'Henderson' was found scratched in at the top of a 300 ft. mast. Will you please ring Ludlow at 12.45.' Henderson was just fifteen.

One advantage of the evacuation was that boys were able to use their initiative not only in the school but in the villages where their Houses were situated. For the first few weeks the local inhabitants were unenthusiastic at this influx of schoolboys from the other end of England and they made it clear that the boys must keep off the farmland. But this suspicion soon broke down. Boys became known individually, they attended the village church, began to help on the farms or in the woods and later began to give entertainments. Perhaps the most ambitious of these was the concert party, mostly from Sanderson's, who called themselves 'The Shropshire Lads'. They stayed on at the beginning of the Christmas holidays in 1942 and gave entertainments in the villages of Brimfield, Richard's Castle, Little Hereford and Caynham. The village halls were packed despite the prognostications of one villager who, pointing to the extra benches remarked, 'You won't need those; we 'aven't 'ad a show here for five years and there was only twenty five people come'. Most of the programme was written and composed by the performers themselves. As these included Royce Ryton, the playwright, and James (Jan) Morris, it was a talented cast. Curiously enough it was Morris and not Ryton who wrote the short play *This is London*, which formed the [...] part of the entertainment. It was a triumphant success and collected [...] for the Red Cross Prisoners of War Fund.

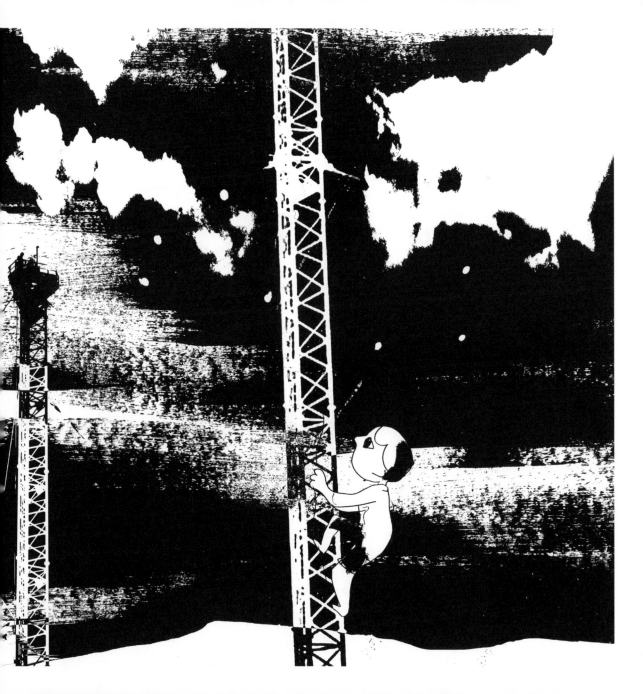

Two of the transmitters were repurposed in an attempt to jam the radio-guidance signals of V-2 rockets, a method later found to be ineffectual.

'The same masts are still in use,' an engineer at Woofferton told me. 'They've been painted a few times, but Henderson's name may still be up there.' We talked about Titterstone too, and when I told him how the Kremlin Inn got its name, he said, 'Oh, that was probably us; the BBC used to broadcast from Woofferton in Russian.'

Carry on, B4362, left at Orleton on to the B4361. Here, Mr Bach, a farmer, had died and left instructions that a certain oak in his meadows should never be cropped or felled in his lifetime. His son continued the tradition, but after his death the estate devolved to his sister, 'whose husband not regarding the aforesaid Will, fell'd the said tree and sold it to the Minister of the Parish, who cut from the Crop nine Foot of the Body to make a nut to his Cider-mill.'

The minister and labourers returned to the tree a day or two later in search of more usable wood. The tree began all of a sudden to move of its own volition. The men retreated, hearing a great crash. The tree had righted itself, its roots back in the hole from which it had been pulled, refusing its death, where, as of October 1734 it still stood.

Now: back on the B4362, right, then right, then left up the drive towards Croft Castle. Managed by the National Trust, the estate was held by the Croft dynasty as far back as the eleventh century. The family fell in and out of grace with monarchs, parliamentarians, nobles and landowners until Sir Archer Croft, going bankrupt in 1746 after the South Sea Bubble burst in 1720, lost the estate to iron master Richard Knight, who sold it to Ludlow MP Somerset Davies in 1783, who sold it again and so on until the Croft family reclaimed and restored the estate in 1923.

Sir James Herbert Croft, rowing captain, hunter, socialite, car enthusiast (in 1936, he was a passenger in a car driven by William James Lysley, 'who was alleged to have travelled through a Cirencester road at more than 50 mph ... exceeding the speed limit in a built-up area') is buried one mile north-northwest of the family church and graveyard, on a promontory looking down into a valley of sweet chestnuts in the estate's woodland on Bircher Common.

CAPTAIN SIR
JAMES HERBERT
CROFT
11TH BARONET
OF CROFT CASTLE
MAY 24TH 1907
AUGUST 15TH 1941.

THEY SHALL NOT
GROW OLD AS WE.
THAT ARE HERE GROW
OLD. AGE SHALL NOT
WEARY THEM NOR
THE YEARS DECAY.

BARONET FOUND SHOT
Asked For Rag To Clean His Revolver

Capt. Sir James Herbert Croft, of Croft Castle, Kingsland, Hereford, died at an Ayrshire hotel soon after he had been found wounded in his room on Friday. Shortly before he had asked for a rag with which to clean his revolver.

Sir James was 34, and was the eleventh baronet, succeeding his father, who was killed in action at the Dardanelles, in 1915. The title passes to an uncle, Mr. Hugh Matthew Fiennes Croft, who is 67, and whose home is at Salisbury Court, Uralla, New South Wales.

For three years in succession Sir James was coxswain of the Oxford eight.

CRAG TRAGEDY
Student Killed On

IN
LOVING MEMORY
KATHERINE AGNES
WIFE OF
SIR HERBERT ARCHER CROFT
10TH BARONET OF CROFT CASTLE
SHE DIED IN HER SLEEP
ON THE NIGHT OF NOV. 30TH 1966
AGED 88 YEARS.
ALSO
OF HER DAUGHTER
ELINOR
14TH FEBRUARY 1904
19TH FEBRUARY 1985

ANGELS OF GLORY ANGELS OF LIGHT
SINGING TO WELCOME THE PILGRIMS OF THE NIGHT

RIP

IN
PROUD AND LOVING
MEMORY OF
SIR HERBERT ARCHER CROFT,
10TH BARONET.
BORN SEPTEMBER 5, 1868,
HIGH SHERIFF OF HEREFORDSHIRE 1911
ENLISTED IN THE
HEREFORDSHIRE REGIMENT
AUGUST 4, 1914,
CAPTAIN SEPTEMBER 12.
KILLED IN ACTION IN GALLIPOLI
AUGUST 1915

IN
PROUD AND LOVING
MEMORY OF
JAMES HERBERT CROFT,
11TH BARONET
BORN MAY 24 1907
1ST SON OF HERBERT ARCHER CROFT
ENLISTED IN THE
HEREFORDSHIRE REGIMENT 1939
CAPTAIN N° 1 COMMANDO
SPECIAL SERVICE 1939
BATTLE OF NORWAY
AND OTHER BATTLES
KILLED ON ACTIVE SERVICE
AUGUST 13, 1941

James's death fell four days after the twenty-sixth anniversary of his father's death. Sir Herbert Archer Croft had landed in Galipoli as part of the Herefordshire Regiment on August 9. When it came time to advance, the battalion moved through the holly scrub under artillery and sniper fire. In the newspapers, after the failed offensive, Croft was listed as lost, presumed dead, at age forty-six, when James was eight.

Like his father, James was recorded as having died in active service.

When Tim and I were little, Mum and Dad would bring us here, park the car in a lay-by to avoid paying the entrance fee, then walk us down into the estate's woods, landscaped in the eighteenth century. There were millponds and follies, plantations of sweet chestnut, beech, oak, pine, and sleeping James Croft.

Memories of these woods – pond-dipping, mud-running, grave-visiting, absurdly bucolic pictures – form the scaffolding of my childhood identity. We were a family as any other, thoroughly unaware that the place was a human-made landscape, oblivious to the history of wealth, power, privilege and tragedy to which it was witness.

Do you like my new hair?

Back in the hospice, Dad's responses become drowsier and wearier, though at first he retains his comic timing – an old joke from Penny, my godmother, elicits a dreamy head-shake right on cue; when we do the crossword together, Dad twitches as John, Penny's husband, starts to read out a clue.

And this is how we wait, with the sound of his respirator heaving and clicking, heaving and clicking, while he sleeps more and more soundly. My cousin Ewan – big, tall, warm, friendly – is a comforting presence. Janet, Dad's sister, is stoic. Mum's strength is remarkable, but we can see her pain.

It is weirdly tranquil, warm and safe, in this little room. The spring, slightly early, begins to unfurl outside the patio doors in his room, a cherry tree starting to swell with blossom, the daffodils waving in the wet breezes, basking in the sudden sun.

Dynasties

May 2015, Exmouth. It is raining full rain, falling on everything – umbrellas, flowers outside supermarkets, pavements, people and seagulls. We seek shelter in the covered market, walking amongst neon toys, functional clothing, secondhand music, the smells of greasy-spoon cafés and the cold, sweet scent of meat at the butcher's. At Martian Records, we click-clack through the CD racks, remarking on bargains and marvelling at the songs of our childhoods being sold extra-cheap. The rain drums on the corrugated roof, the rain drips in the loading bay.

Afterwards, we head to the station, taking the subway under an empty main road. It feels a bit like we're on a teenage date, giddily hanging out, watching the buses out back and waiting for our train.

We catch the 12.23 to Exeter Central. Some squaddies get on at Lympstone, disciplined muscles, disciplined haircuts, bristling with faintly menacing weekend cheer. I want to find fault in their machismo; but I was a weedy nineteen-year-old and I am weedy thirty-one-year-old and I'm not sure if it is them or me that is the problem.

During the first half of 1994, Dad was working at the London Air Terminal Control Centre at Heathrow. He'd spend the weekdays living at the Ramada Hotel at the airport, then come home to Shropshire on the weekends bringing back exotic items like hotel soaps and emery boards and hotel shampoo. I remember staying at the hotel once, seeing how Dad knew all the staff, the waiters, waitresses, cooks and concierges. I was so impressed.

We eventually started looking for houses nearer London so Dad didn't have to live in a hotel, and on my eleventh birthday, in the middle of 1994, we finally waved goodbye to Caynham, to the old Court, to the Camp, to Titterstone Clee Hill, to our friends, and moved to Marlow, a weird commuter town about twenty miles from Heathrow.

The Exe estuary is grey. Here an oystercatcher, there a turnstone, bobbing boats. The train speeds and slows through half a dozen stops. In another carriage a man plays a guitar. We pull through a steep-banked valley, whose high sides flash green through the fogged-up windows. As the terraced houses begin to poke above the brambles, we pass under a brick bridge and into the station. We disembark into a humid crowd, and squeeze through the turnstiles onto Queen Street.

I left home in 2001, moving to Exeter to study Geography at the university. In my first year I lived in halls of residence: Sixties brick-built caves with sweaty walls and sandpaper carpets, unfixed on the bare floor, and a six-foot-three-inch-tall roommate.

'Reminds me of my room in Broadmoor,' joked his five-foot-tall, five-foot-muscle-wide father on our first day. That night we cooked an oven pizza in a microwave and my university career began.

Dad and I shared trips up and down the M4, Marlow to Exeter, at the beginning and end of terms. We got to know the service stations well: Sedgemoor, Bridgwater, Tiverton. At Taunton Deane, we'd sit at a Costa Coffee and watch nobody buy anything from Dr Beak's chicken shop opposite. We agreed one day, before I finished university, we would go and get a bucket there. We never did.

It was on those weird journeys that we got to know each other, or at least adjust our relationship a bit more. Rites of passage and all that. We talked and listened to music. We spent time alone together in a way we didn't otherwise.

Ali and I head to an underground bar called the Cavern for breakfast. I used to come here for gigs and sweaty ceilings and bruised elbows, pound-a-pint on some gut-rot, and a decade later the slippery steps, that faint smell of drains, those posters, are all still the same. It's comforting. We take a rickety seat and behind us a young couple appear. One of them goes off to order.

'My girlfriend said you did burgers.'

'All our food is vegetarian.'

'Since how long?'

He returns; 'Babe, I need meat.'

They opt for milkshakes.

There are two ladies taking selfies over miniature bottles of white wine.

We walk off our breakfast – WH Smith and St Pancras Church, Herbies on Mary Arches Street, and the oast house restaurant round the corner where I once ate veal. We pause at the railings overlooking St Bartholomew's cemetery. Below us the land slips steeply away into grasses and yews and headstones and blackbirds and dog-shit bins.

The tour continues: Fore Street, South Street, Oxfam, Cathedral Yard, Cathedral Green. Buried in Exeter Cathedral is Thomas Hill Peregrine Furye Lowe, the Shropshire-born former Dean of Exeter. He had married Ellen Lucy Pardoe, his neighbour, on February 24 1808, a Wednesday, in Ludlow, and by 1820 he was vicar at Grimley, Worcestershire, before becoming Rector at Holy Trinity, Exeter, in 1837. He gained the office of Dean of Exeter in 1839, and was Vicar between 1840 and 1843 at Littleham. Ellen died on June 17 1843 aged fifty-eight and Thomas held the Deanery of Exeter until his own death on January 17 1861, aged seventy-nine.

When the walkers of the Woolhope Club finished their walk across Titterstone Clee in 1855, it was to Ellen's childhood home of Nash Court about four miles east-southeast of Caynham on the slopes of Clee that they retired for an 'elegant déjeuner' hosted by her nephew George. According to Bagshaw's 1851 *History, Gazetteer & Directory of Shropshire*, Nash Court was a 'handsome brick mansion ... surrounded by beautiful pleasure grounds, and [a] park ... richly timbered,' built on the top of a hill.

The Pardoe family had held the estate since at least the mid-eighteenth century, when George Dansey Pardoe and his wife Ellen Dansey Pardoe had moved from Cleeton, where George was vicar, to the small hamlet of Nash.

The Pardoe family history reached all the way back to the Battle of Bosworth in 1485, after which their allegiance to a Welsh prince named Thomas ap Adam saw the family rewarded with an ascent through both the ecclesiastical and social ranks in the Welsh Marches. By the seventeenth century, the Pardoe family came to own the manors of Nash, Cleeton St Mary, Credden, Faintree, Burford, and property across Shropshire.

Nash Court was only a short walk from my friend Mark's house, in the countryside we prowled as ten-year-olds. We would wade through rivers and duck barbed wire and camouflage ourselves from farmers in their tractors.

By the time the Woolhopians arrived at Nash Court, George Dansey Pardoe had left the family home to his son George, becoming vicar at the village of Hopton Castle where, in February 1644, thirty parliamentarian soldiers from England and Wales, under instruction from the owner Robert Wallop, dug in against a Royalist army of some five hundred soldiers under the command of Sir Michael Woodhouse.

The ensuing siege lasted for three weeks. The account given by Samuel More, the Parliamentarian commanding officer, written during his imprisonment after the attack, tells of how the Royalists were beaten back, time after time, and how he had refused on more than one occasion petitions to surrender. Finally, on March 14 1644, after a day of relentless cannon fire, Woodhouse's forces breached the encampment and More's soldiers were routed to the castle keep.

The soldiers became trapped; 'the castle consisting but of one room below and another above, we had no space to countermine, and our stairs were up, being close to the door where the barricade was, and removing Mr Gregory's provision and stuff in, both Mr Phillips myself and six more did plainly hear their working under us.' The Royalists lit a fire at the base of the tower, and realising that they were finally defeated, the Roundheads surrendered to Colonel Woodhouse's mercy.

More was arrested and taken to Ludlow Castle. Captain Priamus Davies, stationed at nearby Brampton, wrote how at Hopton, command was given that the remaining Parliamentarians 'should be bound two and three, [and] stripped naked as ever they were born, it being about the beginning of March very cold and many of them sore wounded in defending their own works. There they remained about an hour until the word was given that they should be left to the mercy of the common soldiers, who presently fell upon them, wounding them grievously, and drove them into a cellar unfinished, wherein was stinking water, the house being on fire over them, when they were every man of them presently massacred; amongst whom Phillips, a young gentleman of sweet and comely person and admirable parts, suffered.'

In a later correspondence with Phillips' brother, More relates how their captors 'swore at Philips and stabbed him presently; all the rest, being twenty-five, were killed with clubs or such things after they were stripped naked. Two maids they stripped to their smocks and cut them, but some helped them to escape.'

The soldiers' bodies have never been recovered.

PETER BR...

By Order of the Council of the National Association of Boys' Clubs

NASH COURT, LUDLOW, SALOP

GEORGIAN COUNTRY HOUSE   ...oses or administra...

George Dansey Pardoe lived out his days at Hopton Castle as a clergyman, preaching near the sleeping garrison. His two sisters had married into the church: Ellen married Thomas Lowe, whilst Maria married Rev Richard Powell of Munslow at Tenbury in 1807.

Maria died in 1819. At their church, a sarcophagus was placed against the south wall of the chancel and inscribed:

'Sacred to the memory of Maria Powell, the deeply lamented wife of the Rev Richard Powell, Rector of this parish, who departed this life in the humble hope of a blessed mortality, Sept 27, 1819, aged 32 years, leaving three surviving children, and an afflicted husband, by whom this monument is erected.

Cara Maria, vale; veniat felicius ævum

Quando interum tecum (sim modo dignus) ero!

Puellarum elegantissima, flore venustatis abrepta, vale! Heu quanto minus est cum reliquis versari quàm tui meminisse!

Beloved Maria, farewell! I long for happier times

when (as long as I prove worthy) I will be with you again!

Farewell! Most graceful of girls, Bloom of Delight snatched away

Alas! How hard it is to dwell here with the remnants and only a memory of you.'

George Pardoe took holy orders and became vicar at Cleeton St Mary, where he was instrumental in the redevelopment of the village. In the period in between the Woolhope meal and his death in 1884, he concentrated his efforts on the village, endowing and building a school, four almshouses, St Mary's Church and the rectory, downslope from Newfound Well, and in 1871 he installed a stained-glass mirror in his father's honour at Hopton Church.

George's nephew, George Owen, became vicar of Hyssington, Montgomeryshire, in 1874. He married Letitia Louisa Southey in 1876, and in 1877, they had a son, George Southey Pardoe who followed his father and grandfather and great-grandfather into the clergy. He held a vicarage at Muncaster Castle in Cumbria, and eventually travelled overseas with the military during World War I as a Chaplain.

He was killed in action on October 15 1918, in Palestine.

In the Guildhall shopping centre the floor squeaks under our wet soles.

Our adventure done, we head back on the train, back past the estuary. There's no bus at Exmouth and the taxi to my parents' house in Budleigh Salterton smells of stale cigarettes and our wet clothes.

Back at Mum and Dad's, we hibernate. My parents retired here from Marlow in 2011, and found a new lease of life walking on the coast, going on holiday, taking up hobbies.

I moved away from Exeter in 2004, spent some time living in Cornwall and then Cardiff with its dhustone docks, before moving once again, this time to Bristol. Thomas Lowe's successor, Charles Ellicott, served as Dean of Exeter until 1863 when he became the Bishop of the United Sees of Gloucester and Bristol, before the bishopric was separated out and George Forrest Browne, a committed climber and speleologist, became Bishop of Bristol in 1897.

I have lived here for the last thirteen years.

It's the longest I've ever lived anywhere.

The vigil

Things carry on, opening out across an endless expanse of space and time. It might only have been a handful of days, but for us it is one single moment, stretched like cling film across the uncomfortable chairs, the adjustable bed, my Dad's sleeping form, the flowers, the vase, the pens and the paper, the half-finished crossword, plastic glasses of water, chest of drawers, doorhandles, us, our hollow, hand-touching, story-telling forms.

Ewan goes out for a cigarette.

A nurse comes in.

A nurse goes out.

Ewan returns.

Our routine becomes get up in the morning, eat toast, drive to the hospice, sit, eat lunch at his bedside, remain as long as possible. Not on autopilot, not sleepwalking, totally present, simply surviving, living one breath to the next, the universe on pause.

We never want to leave at night, and when we do go home we sleep only lightly, one ear open for the phone ringing. We talk about how hard it is, how it feels like we have been doing this routine forever, even though it has barely been a working week. We can't imagine ever not having done it, or ever not doing it. I can't imagine leaving him or him leaving us.

The vigil is exhausting.

A chace for deare

One night, I was driving us all back to Mum and Dad's house from the hospice. The sky was clear, damp roads, cool air. We were shattered and quiet and deeply tired, moving in a dream, jet-lag-slow, fizzy bodies, cold fingertips.

As we came into Budleigh Salterton, down the hill where the speed limit drops from forty to thirty, we sensed motion in the trees to our left. A crashing of tawny roe deer became visible, keeping pace with us. They were startling to us, ragged as our nerves were, but they were very, very beautiful. It was a weird moment, feeling primal, connected, sharing amygdalan responses in the dark with these other animals that weren't us, moving in the moonlight.

'Do you think that was your Dad, as a deer?' Ali asked later.

I paused and then I replied, 'I think it was the universe telling us that no matter what happens, everything will be OK.' But I wasn't convinced by my own response, and as I fell asleep that night I started, in the anxious interstices, to think that maybe Ali could have been right.

VII.—From Miss Berta Hurly.

"Waterbeach Vicarage, Cambridge, *February*, 1890.

"In the spring and summer of 1886 I often visited a poor woman called Evans, who lived in our parish, Caynham. She was very ill with a painful disease, and it was, as she said, a great pleasure when I went to see her; and I frequently sat with her and read to her. Towards the middle of October she was evidently growing weaker, but there seemed no immediate danger. I had not called on her for several days, and one evening I was standing in the dining-room after dinner with the rest of the family, when I saw the figure of a woman dressed like Mrs. Evans, in large apron and muslin cap, pass across the room from one door to the other, where she disappeared. I said, 'Who is that?' My mother said, 'What do you mean?' and I said, 'That woman who has just come in and walked over to the other door.' They all laughed at me, and said I was dreaming, but I felt sure it was Mrs. Evans, and next morning we heard she was dead.

"Berta Hurly."

When it happened

Dad died the next day, two hours after the morning high water at Topsham, at the beginning of March 2017.

There is a tendency, the nurses had told us, for terminally ill people to try and slip away when you're not there; you can hold a twenty-four-hour vigil three days in a row, nip out for a wee, and find them gone.

Dad, typically, was no different. While Ali and I were driving to the hospice, my family were being ushered out of his room so the nurses could change his clothes and his bedding. While this was happening, he started very suddenly to change his breathing, a sure sign, the nurses had warned us previously, that he was at the end of his life. Everyone rushed back to his room, except my mum who was in the toilet and nearly missed the whole thing, and us, driving in Dad's old car, who did.

We had been in Tesco's buying food so that everyone camped out at his bedside could have something other than hospice baguettes to eat for lunch. We were on the Topsham Road, waiting at the lights that filter traffic onto Barrack Road to change. A text message arrived from my brother. We were two minutes from the hospice but for some reason I replied telling him we'd be another fifteen minutes. The traffic lights changed. We pulled away. We turned right onto Barrack Road. He died. We turned right onto Dryden Road, left into the hospital grounds, left again into the hospice car park.

My cousin, my aunt, my godparents were standing outside the hospice looking grey-faced. I drove the car into a parking space straight ahead of me. I turned the engine off, took the key out of the ignition, and started to open the door before I had even put on the handbrake. Even now I can feel the change in momentum of the silent Honda, the lurch, the inertia.

We got out. John's arms were crossed.

'He's gone,' he said as we approached. 'He didn't suffer. It was quick.'

I thanked him – squeezed his arm maybe? – and ran inside through the automatic doors, past the reception desk, turned left down the corridor, through the open ward, and into Dad's room, while a beautiful Devon spring unfurled two weeks early outside – sun candling the daffodils, the tree cherry-blossomed.

Twelve
March

Chapel of Rest

Alone in a dim room. Spotlit bed. Clean t-shirt. Covers pulled up to armpits. Arms tucked under. Face yellow. Teeth exposed. Eyes open. Stretched thin. Head tilt towards me. Rigour hinted. Stained glass above twinkles colour where his colour is gone. Except for the yellow.

It is six years and four months since we moved away from Shropshire.

I don't want to go to school and my A-levels are going moderately beigely: sure the grades are fine, but all the teachers are saying, 'He could be so much more if only he would try harder.'

I'm in a relationship with someone whom I undoubtedly care for a great deal, but in that first-love way where the combination of lust, friendship, chaos, growth, ambition and playing at being a grown-up gets very, very confused; two kids with broken hearts, trying to understand young love's intense contradictions.

I don't know what I want. Or rather, I do, but I have neither the experiential common sense nor the emotional vocabulary to work out how to articulate it, let alone go about getting it.

Dad and I have been having a bit of a testy time. He is given at the moment to be snappy, short-tempered. Because I am at the centre of my world at this age, I think it is him being unreasonable (and not the unreasonably long hours he spends working and commuting to and from Gatwick where he is now based) that leads to the altercations that are fraying his already frayed tolerance.

It is Monday October 16 2000, at about seven o'clock in the evening. I am sat on my bed, trying to learn a song on the guitar. I'm not very good. Dad knocks on my bedroom door and comes in. He has a small exercise book in his hand.

He sits next to me and starts talking to me softly. It is a tone of voice I don't recognise, not because Dad is not soft (he is) or is usually harsh (he is never harsh) but because, I think, he is trying really hard to do something that isn't easy for him.

He shows me the book. In it are written some poems. He says he wrote them when he was my age, at that point in life when he had just left home, was confused and angry and excited and scared, just like I was.

As I look at the poems he speaks to me about making hard decisions, and being happy, and doing what was right for me. I don't think he even means the school work or my decisions about university; I think he means for me to stop fighting myself, and make the changes I need to make, for myself.

I sit quietly with the book after he leaves, knowing that my relationship with him has changed, gently but significantly.

Shut the door, quick, don't let this be your last view, burned on my retina; now writing, nearly crying, while nine hundred years ago, a boy breaks through the wall of the forgotten tomb, lost all these years near Much Wenlock, and finds the body of St Milburga, incorrupted, two hundred years gone and as pure as the day she was buried.

Is he still there?
      In the hospice?

No, he's not.
      I keep expecting him to be here instead.
            But he isn't.

The blue sky is here, the morning dew is here,
      the blossom and the pollen is here, so is Spring, and so are we.

But where is he?

The event of death

While the boundary between life and death is crossed in an instant, the duration of death is something experienced differently for those left living. When we speak of the death of a loved one, and speak of their absence, we also speak of what it is to experience someone's passing: the hours of gritted teeth in hospitals or care homes, in houses or at roadsides, the persistence of the sadness and the rage, and how it goes on and on.

For us, the event of our own death begins before we are born and carries on for hours, days, weeks, months, centuries after our last breath is expelled. It has its own barely knowable logic. The event of death is crass, jocular, spiteful, benign; it is niggling doubts about a cough; it is canteen sandwiches and empty wardrobes, smart shirts on other men; it is 'see, I told you I was ill!'

The event of death is only sudden in the way a thunderstorm is sudden; in the instant when we confront the deluge caused by an abrupt downpour, we forget the changes in air pressure, the bridling of weather fronts, the heating and cooling of land masses, the electrical charge, all necessary to birth a storm.

The event of death demands administration. Forms and paperwork and things to sign and policies to cancel and call centres to negotiate with – of course I can help you, sir, I'm so sorry for your loss. The event of death is an introduction to carefully archived evidence of a life lived, or a drawer full of receipts, unlabelled keys, out-of-date tinned sweets, and a picture postcard from the Lake District sent by someone called Angie, whom nobody can remember.

The event of death makes absence corporeal. We accrue those absences throughout our lives, and just as we feel the resonance of deaths that happened before we were even born, our deaths will be felt long after we are gone. The event of death always leaves its scent, like a lingering fart left by the Grim Reaper after he has sent his quarry across the Styx, and all you can do is stand around sniffing.

We naturalise death's rhythms, for, 'as life comes in with the flow, so it goes with the ebb,' writes Christina Hole; '...no-one can die until the tide begins to run out.' Creatures of the moon, all of us, and I've worked in bars on enough full moons to believe that there's something to that.

'The domestic creatures must share the family sorrow,' writes Burne. 'The bees are told the news, and often put into mourning, the rooks are warned. At Church Stretton the farm-horses are not worked, at Ludlow they say the fowls hide themselves all day, until the funeral.'

We'll do what we can to ease our collusion in the event of death, too. Burne reports how, 'It is held in Shropshire that every person who sees a corpse should lay his hand upon it: if not, he will dream of it afterward and can it be that this touch was once intended as a solemn proof that the visitor was guiltless of having caused the death, either by violence or by spells; and that whoever shrank back from the test was supposed to be liable to be haunted in his dreams by the dead man, as if he had been a murderer?'

What about the sinne-eaters who, to ease the passage of the dead, and rid the living of their ghostly persistence, took upon themselves, as Aubrey reported in the seventeenth century, 'all the Sinnes of the Defunct'?

John Bagford, in a letter dated February 1 1714, and quoted by Burne, writes, 'In Shropshire ... when a person dyed, there was notice given to an old Sire (for so they called him) who presently repaired to the place where the deceased lay, and stood before the door of the house, when some of the Family came out and furnished him with a Cricket, on which he sat down facing the door. Then they gave him a Groat, which he put in his pocket; a Crust of Bread, which he eat; and a full bowle of Ale, which he drank off at a draught. After this, he got up from the Cricket and pronounced, with a composed gesture, the ease and rest of the Soul departed, for which he would pawn his own Soul.'

All of these customs have developed so that the event of death can be understood, or contained, from wreaths in churches, to decking out the streets with tables and chairs on which the pallbearers can rest their burden as they process from the deceased's home to the church.

But the event of death continues, even after the shutters are opened and we have cast the windows wide to let the cold air back into the house, when the candles have gone out, and the chairs in the parlour are set back against the wall, no longer required as a stand for the coffin we recently use to swaddle our dearly departed, as peacefully as could be achieved.

Then, one day, we were walking past the funeral home behind Saint Paul's, a nineteenth-century church built for the burgeoning congregation of an industrialised south Bristol. Outside the Chapel of Rest, black-suited men and women were loading a coffin into a hearse. The coffin was decorated in laminated plastic which depicted pixelated photographs of flames and roasting chickens. It also bore the words 'Roast Chicken' on its sides and on its lid.

Order of Service

We sit with the celebrant, talking about the mechanics of funeral services. He has a big binder with him. I do not know what is in it.

In 1502 Prince Arthur dies in Ludlow and his body is drawn by a six-horse carriage through Caynham, Hope Bagot, Coreley, Earls Ditton, Hopton Wafers, Catherton and across the River Rea at Ditton in Neen Savage parish, towards Bewdley. It rains heavily, and in places the mud is so bad that oxen have to be drafted in to assist the cortege.

In February 1738 at Leintwardine, Ned of the Toddin digs up his dead mother, his only carer, and brings her home, warms her by the fire, puts her to bed, and asks, 'Why were you so foolish as to die, to go to such a cold hole?'

In June 1994, as we are packing our things in boxes ready to move house, over in Ludlow hundreds of honey bees gather on the outside of a house at the corner of Mill Street and Bell Lane.

It is the day of eighty-five-year-old Margaret Bell's funeral. After her service, which concluded with the hymn 'All Things Bright and Beautiful', the mourners are astonished to see the bees, which happen to have alighted directly opposite the house where Bell had been living for the last twenty-six years.

Margaret Bell was a beekeeper with hives at nearby Leintwardine. The local paper runs a photograph, later reproduced in *Fortean Times* magazine, of Bell's friends standing beneath the bee cluster, laughing, touched, looking upwards.

'I think it's absolutely wonderful that they should stop opposite her house,' Mrs Bell's friend, Sue Walsh, is quoted as saying.

'The bees stayed for about an hour before buzzing off over the rooftop,' concludes the report.

'I believe it would be difficult to meet with any cottage beekeeper,' writes Burne, 'who did not honestly think that his insects were endued with knowledge and sagacity beyond that of the rest of the brute creation and sometimes that of mankind.'

'What music will you play?' asks the celebrant.

Mum pays for the funeral, and receives an obscene amount of supermarket loyalty points in return.

The funeral

The funeral ached in the way that they do. Throughout, it rained heavy but mistily, followed by bright sunshine and blue skies, then bruise-black skies and more rain.

'About the year 1854,' writes Burne, 'two little boys were playing in the fields at Aston Botterel, under the Brown Clee Hill, when a sudden shower of rain made them take shelter in a neighbouring "coppy". Soon, however, the sun shone out, and one of the boys (the son of a labourer, with whose master the other was staying) said, "When it rains and the sun shines, the cuckoo is going to heaven".'

On the way to the wake at the Thirsty Farmer, we saw on the verges and in the hedges on the country lanes that it had been hailing chickpea- and baked-bean-sized hailstones.

At the pub, we chatted to his former colleagues, some of his friends; some of my old friends came, too. I looked at old photos of Dad I'd never seen before that his friends brought along – one of Dad in the back of the van he owned as a teenager with some friends, one of whom was named Blodwyn; and one of a nineteen-year-old Dad at a ping-pong table. Another man at the funeral told me about how they'd spent teenage evenings in hostel rooms while out on training exercises, using an old cassette recorder to record versions of *Monty Python* and *Fawlty Towers* sketches.

I learned how Dad had changed the lives of the people he worked with, first in small ways, and then as he gradually changed jobs, moving towards management, had helped those people around him to grow and develop, sometimes with a nudge, sometimes a push. It was a side of him I did not and could not know, but it made me proud to hear these stories.

The wake ended and we filtered away from the pub to walk on the beach at Budleigh. The rest of the day felt angular and odd.

Gran, Dad's mum, was the first person in my family I really remember dying and the first funeral I attended, my grandfather having predeceased her when I was five, and my only memory of that was being in a park with my Mum and seeing a rat by some water.

I was twelve when Gran died, some eighteen months after we moved away from Shropshire. She had Parkinson's. The family story goes that she always attributed the development of her condition to a fall in the snow in 1960.

Like many people who are ill with things that distort how they look and sound and which you encounter when you are a child, I took it as a given that this was Gran, this was who and how she was. By the time she died, I was only just starting to understand that she was somehow more than how the illness presented itself, that the aesthetic of illness obscures things, like someone's sense of humour, history, strengths, experience.

The night before her funeral, my family had stayed in a hotel – a Travelodge or something similar – outside Maidstone. My brother and I were sharing a room of our own. He was fourteen and had been afforded this privilege, no doubt, on the assumption that he would look after me and that we would behave.

We were on the ground floor, facing the back of the hotel. That night we opened the curtains so the electric light of our room spread out like a frame across the patch of ground behind the hotel, bounded by a fence and some bald trees. A thin layer of snow shone. It was like another planet. Without discussing it, we quietly put on our coats and climbed out of the window. The snowballs flew and our hands grew cold, duking it out with the last of the snow or the best of the icy dirt, under a new moon.

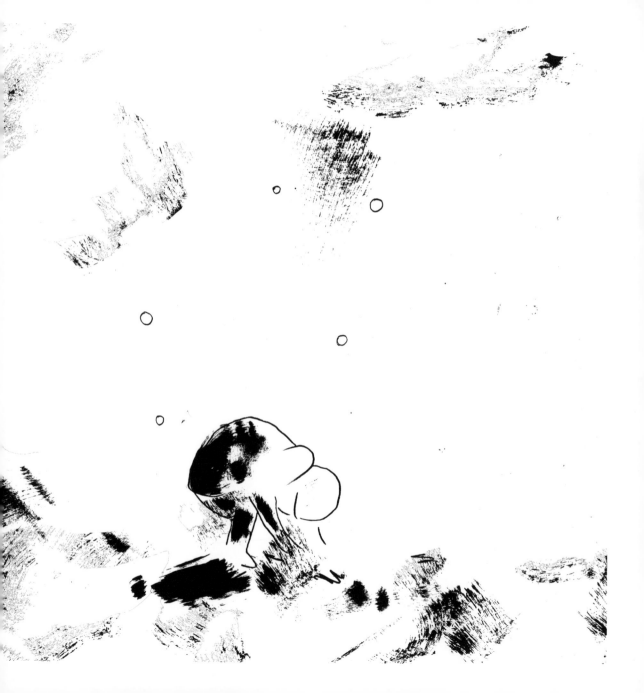

Family and friends of beekeeper Margaret Bell pose beneath the bees in Bell Lane, Ludlow. From left: Sue Walsh, Cynthia Francis, Jean Bell and Don Faulkner.

ST IG

e
ll
ad
n
is
her
g to

ye.
al on 7
obvi-
mourn-
1994.

DIG
BEAT

to the Navy.
derwater
s and marine
nned scuba gear
te. The sound
anically steady
was intermittent,
uous. Whales, dol-
d submarine-con-
onar generated by
ll ruled out

WE'RE
LOSING
MOON

Thirteen
Where?

The lie of the land

Knowledge of those who have gone before us, wrote Alfred Watkins in his 1925 book, *The Old Straight Track*, 'is only to be gleaned from three types of evidence; firstly and chiefly from what exists or is recorded on or in the earth of the work or remains of man of that period. Secondly, from what can be gleaned and surmised in place-names and words, for it is often forgotten that words were spoken in Britain for more centuries before they were written down than there have been centuries of written record, and there are indications that many word elements come down through both periods. Thirdly, from folk-lore legends; lingering fragments of fact disguised by an overlay of generations of imaginings.'

Watkins, entrepreneur, brewer, photography pioneer, businessman, Herefordian of note, argued that in prehistory, until at least the arrival of the Romans, the land – being at first forested and largely impassable except for by human intervention – was hard to navigate. He suggested that the response was to create lines of sight – straight trackways – that aligned natural and manmade features for the purpose of traversing the country. These had domestic, commercial and ritual significance, bringing people to sacred sites or acting as trading routes.

Watkins found his evidence on maps, in place names and in the alignment of geographic features, such as contours, lakes, rivers and human-made features: holloways, stone circles, barrows and latterly churches. He called these lines 'leys'.

Titterstone Clee Hill, he suggested, was one node in a network of leys, a meaningful prominence in the visual and spiritual geography of early humankind.

In a lecture titled *Early British Trackways, Moats, Mounds, Camps and Sites*, given to the Woolhope Club at Hereford in September 1921, Watkins discussed the etymological root of the name Titterstone.

'Totnor, Totteridge, Tothill and Twt,' he said, 'indicate tumps, and they are all sighting tumps on leys. Mr Wood (who has come very near discovering the ley) also – in Woolhope Transactions for 1919 – connects Titterstone, Clee Hill with the word Tot or Toot. Tooting and Tottenham are London forms of the word. Rosemary Topping (English Bicknor) is a much prettier name for a sighting tump.'

Like a lighthouse, suggested Watkins, Titterstone Clee was used as a means of planning out the direction of leys, even if ultimately such paths fell short of the hill itself.

Charles Henry Hartshorne, a Shropshire-born antiquarian and clergyman, thought Titterstone significant, too. In the Autumn of 1837 while walking on the hill, he was struck by a large erratic, which he took to be a rocking stone, an improbably balanced boulder that could be moved by the lightest of touches.

Forced to leave Shropshire before having a chance to confirm his suspicions, he spent the following months looking elsewhere for evidence that would support his theory. He writes in his 1841 book, *Salopia antiqua: or, an enquiry from personal survey into the 'druidical,' military, and other early remains in Shropshire and the north Welsh borders*, that although he had found that 'there exists a traditionary account of a former rocking stone on this eminence... I knew it would be in vain to seek for any account that would tend to confirm these views, as all our early remains in Shropshire have singularly escaped the attention of antiquarian enquiries.'

He began to look for evidence, as Wood and Watkins would some eighty years later, in the etymology of the name. 'It appeared,' he claimed, 'that the Titterstone itself had derived its name from the Islandic *tittra*, which signifies *to tremble*.' There was, he felt, 'no longer any room left for doubting that this stone, or at least some other upon the same eminence had been the means of distinguishing the mountain itself.'

While vicar of Leamington, Warwickshire, in 1838 – a post he did not enjoy, writing to his friend Albert Way of a climate, 'which everything intellectual shuns' – he returned to Titterstone Clee. This time, he took with him a team of local men who under his supervision spent two hours clearing the stones that had gathered at the rocking stone's base. Despite a fit of self-doubt – brought, on he imagined, from the exertion of the ascent – when the locals had finished their work, he felt vindicated. He christened his newly uncovered rocking stone *The Titterstone*, and proudly drew a pencil sketch of the tumble of rocks and the wobbly stone that crowned them.

to Mr. H., and he felt so grateful for the kind reception he had met with from him, that he took the opportunity of expressing his gratitude in a series of very beautiful Latin verses.—This elegant compliment led to a friendship of the most honourable and disinterested nature between the two gentlemen. Shortly after the first interview, Mr. Hebers entreated Mr. H. to come and pay him a visit at his house in London. The latter gentleman accepted his invitation, and came to town. Mr. H. knowing his friend was of a decidedly literary turn of mind, took every opportunity of introducing him to those literary circles, most congenial to men of letters; in a word, he treated him as a brother. They dined together at the house of a common acquaintance, and the Learned Gentleman supposed the viper, who had spread the poison complained of, had imbibed it there. In the August of 1825, Mr. Hebers quitted England, but previousl he had introduced Mr. Hartshorn to the Earl o Guildford. This Nobleman having occasion t make a tour in the September following, he pr

Hartshorne's own route to Clee was a strange one. He was born an only child on March 17 1802 in Broseley, Shropshire, a town we knew well, it being where some friends of my parents lived in a small terraced cottage; I remember late-night drives home, Leonard Cohen cassette playing, country darkness in the thick hedges outside.

Hartsthorne's father, John, known locally as the Ironmaster, died in 1805, just as the Industrial Revolution was really getting sootily into its sway in their town and over what would later be called the Ironbridge Gorge, in Madeley and Coalbrookdale. His early death left the family financially constrained and as he grew older Charles realised he would be unable to pursue his ambition to study law. Instead, on the advice of Shrewsbury judge Sir James Alan Parkinstead, he turned towards a career in the clergy.

It was also through this association with Parkinstead that Hartshorne came into contact with Richard Heber, a prominent bibliophile and antiquarian. Heber's connections at the British Museum in particular were attractive to Charles, who had begun to express an interest in historical studies.

The two met in March 1821 at the Assizes in Shrewsbury, shortly before Hartshorne left Shropshire to study at Cambridge. The two went on to spend a number of days together in Oxford in July 1821, when Charles was nineteen and Richard was forty-eight. Hartshorne then spent the Christmas of 1823 with Heber and a further two months visiting with him in London in 1824.

Hartshorne travelled to Corfu the following year at the invitation of Frederick North, Fifth Earl of Guildford, undertaking the Grand Tour through Italy, the Middle East and Greece.

Heber left England abruptly for Continental Europe not long after, sending a letter upon reaching Antwerp resigning his post as a Member of Parliament for Oxford University. *The Morning Chronicle* reported later that '[the news] was received [at Oxford] with considerable regret, great efforts having been made by many of the Colleges... to ensure his election. Some of the Fellows expressed themselves with warm and unwarrantable indignation on the subject.'

While Heber and Hartshorne were abroad, *John Bull*, a Tory periodical, published an article on May 14 1826 insinuating that the two men were lovers. The article ran: 'Mr Heber, the late Member for Oxford University, will not return to this country for some time – the backwardness of the season renders the Continent more congenial to some constitutions. The complaint for which Mr Heber has been recommended to travel,' the article continued, 'is said to have been produced by an over-addiction to *Hartshorn*.'

The implication by innuendo of a sexual relationship between the two men took its toll. Many of Heber's allies turned against him in his absence; when Sir Walter Scott, a friend and fellow book collector, learned of the rumours, he wrote in his journal on June 25 1826, 'God, God, whom shall we trust! Here is learning, wit, gaiety of temper, high station in society and compleat reception every where all at once debased and lost.'

Two weeks later, in a letter to his son-in-law J. G. Lockhart, Scott wrote, 'I think with horror that if he had asked me to let my son go on a trip to the Continent with him or any other such expedition I should have considered it the most fortunate thing in the world.'

Hartshorne returned to England in August 1826 and discovered what had happened. He wrote to Heber in September, and although Heber responded offering financial support for a libel case, he did not return from the mainland. With Heber gone, Hartshorne was left to pursue the magazine in the court that October.

At the trial, Mr Scartlett, representing Hartshorne, stated in his address to the judge, Lord Tenterden, that, 'unfortunately, in the present age, there is such an appetite for slander that one class of public journals lend themselves to the insertion of paragraphs by which the character and reputation of a man who has borne the most unspotted character from his earliest youth, may be blast by a sarcasm, or annihilated by an insinuation.'

'A young man of handsome figure, and grave intelligent countenance,' Hartshorne's character, was argued to the court to be 'unimpeachable', and the 'atrocity of the libel, which, although it had not a shadow of probability to rest upon, was from its very nature injurious to the slandered person, and had, in fact, caused Mr Hartshorne to be cut off from all society except that of his immediate friends.' The allegations, added the *Public Ledger and Daily Advertiser* on Monday 20 November 1826, were 'calculated to blast the laurels gained by many a year's laborious study; ... to throw a mildew on the prospects of both gentlemen during the remaining years of their life.'

Edward Shackell, editor and owner of *John Bull*, was found guilty of defamation and fined £500, but this proved to be a Pyrrhic victory for Hartshorne. He was left in near financial and social ruin. He returned to the clergy and was ordained in 1827 and the following year he became curate of Little Wenlock, marrying Frances Margaretta Kerrich on December 10.

While the specific relationship alluded to in *John Bull* was most likely platonic, rumours about Heber's sexuality had been circulating for some years. His departure for Europe, it would later transpire, had been urged by Home Secretary and future Prime Minister, Robert Peel. Peel had heard accusations of sexual advances that Heber had allegedly made at the Athenaeum Club towards two young men, one of whom was the son of a publishing agent named Mr Fisher.

The rumours left Heber with few allies, as Under-Secretary of State for the Home Office Henry Hobhouse related in a letter he wrote to Heber upon the latter's departure for Europe: 'I think the objective of those with whom I have recently communicated respecting you is to prevent your retaining the place you have filled in English society; and that if that object can be attained without recourse to legal proceedings, there is no disposition to take those steps, to which they would otherwise recur. Under these circumstances you must judge for yourself of the prudence of visiting England, taking into the account that since your departure the facts have (I believe) been imparted to Mr F[isher] ... If you resolve on running the risk, there are cogent reasons, why I should neither be party nor privy to the fact of your being here.'

Sir Walter Scott alluded to the existence of an arrest warrant against Heber being written, though if it existed it was never actioned.

Heber eventually returned to England in 1831 but found himself ostracised. Even the defence offered by his few remaining friends only argued for the validity of his denials; while no corroborating evidence of the Athenaeum incident was ever released, the notion that Heber could be gay – which was most likely the case – was still unconscionable.

He died in seclusion at the age of fifty-nine in London on October 4 1833, apparently of an 'attack on the lungs accompanied by jaundice,' and was buried at Hodnet in Shropshire the following month. Many newspapers published sympathetic obituaries, largely omitting any comment of the scandals. In some, though, the speculation continued. In their obituary, the *North Wales Chronicle* noted how after his return from Europe, Heber was 'evidently broken down in constitution, and his death was the consequence of gradual decay, perhaps produced by a wounded spirit.'

George Burges, an English scholar at Trinity College, Cambridge, shared this judgement in a letter to the *Morning Chronicle*. On having seen Heber a month prior to his death he wrote, 'I can testify to the mere wreck his once manly form and buoyant spirit exhibited, when sinking under the imputations as foul and fake as were ever disseminated by the most scurrilous of papers in its period of bloated prosperity.' His defence, in a letter that rattles with rage, continued; 'so it is in this hypocritical age; a man's fair fame may be whispered away by persons who want the manliness to make a direct charge, but who, breathing only the polluted atmosphere of scandal, must daily blast some character.'

By 1838, Hartshorne had taken up a post at Cogenhoe church in Northamptonshire. He enjoyed the place, finding it 'hoary with grey lichen … the natural abode of an Antiquary,' and it was while here that he wrote his account of his trips to Titterstone.

The chronicle of the Woolhope Club's visit to Titterstone Clee in 1855 makes no mention of a rocking stone. In 1858, *Archaeologia Cambrensis* alludes to 'a heap of enormous stones, no doubt remaining as they were placed by natural causes but which have the appearance of great cromlechs in a state of ruin.'

Hartshorne died suddenly at Holdenby, a private estate in Northamptonshire where he had become Rector, on March 11 1865, a week shy of his sixty-third birthday. Although firsthand accounts seem to fail to mention it again, the suggestion of a Trembling Stone at Clee persisted. *The Circling Year*, published in 1871, noted that 'a rocking-stone and caves upon the Titterstone Clee Hill' were evidence of druidic activity on the hilltop. Charlotte Burne makes passing reference to these speculations, too; Oliver Baker, also refers to the rocking stone as hearsay in his 1888 tourist guide *Ludlow Town and Neighbourhood.*

According to Woolhope member, L. V. Grinsell, the attribution of the creation of rocking stones to druidic activity is one of the great 'red herrings' of archaeology. This was an opinion shared by Hartshorne who wrote: 'They have been called artificial and fabled to have been placed in their state of equipoise by incredible skill and labour ... but of all the fallacies which dreaming antiquaries have echoed from age to age to mislead their followers, this is among the greatest.'

Nonetheless, there's no rocking stone visible today and perhaps Hartshorne, in his eagerness to be looked at with acclaim by the society that had rejected him in his youth, unconsciously recreated a vanished monument that was never there in the first place, reading into the landscape and marking into it the things he felt should have been there all along.

The second of Grinsell's red herrings was Watkins' theory of leys, which has today largely been either dismissed or absorbed into more esoteric areas of scholarship. Building on Watkins' work, new theories emerged which sought to locate a causality for leys. This led – thanks in part to mischievous John Michell and his *View Over Atlantis* – to talk of channels of earth energy that radiate around the word, and into which pre-modern humans were able to tap more readily than we rational, scientific souls. This pointed towards a holistic, international, prehistoric mode of living, balanced between land and sky, and drawn out in arcs around the globe.

Watkins never went that far in his thinking. He writes in his preface to *The Old Straight Track*, 'What really matters in this book is whether it is a humanly designed fact, an accidental coincidence, or a "mare's nest", that mounds, moats, beacons and mark stones fall into straight lines throughout Britain, with fragmentary evidence of trackways on the alignments.'

Mare's nest or not, sighting tump or not, the connection to Titterstone Clee in my version of our family topography is tangible, written into my contract, under my skin, in my bones, lungs. My tump, our tump, here, a sighting point for our own leys. Look now! West, to where my brother lives among the coffee and hummingbirds of San Francisco. Look now! Northeast, over the Pennines to where my Mum's family came from – Sheffield, Leeds, Otley, Harewood, colliers, blacksmiths, stonemasons, farmers. Look now! Arcing south across Norfolk's great flat expanse, wet Doggerland, towards East Anglia, Bury St Edmunds, where my parents once lived, where they met our godparents, now south, south to Dover where I was born, to Maidstone, Dad's family home, generations of agricultural labourers. Look now! Southwest towards Bristol, Exeter, Falmouth, where I carved out little bits of me in the little bits of land where I lived. It's as if all roads lead here, or at least I could trick myself into thinking that they do.

'Where shall we go on our honeymoon, John?' sings the singer on the hill.

'Why up the lane and back again.'

The goodbye

In early August 2017, my Mum, my brother and I decamped for two days and a night to Shropshire. Mum came up to Bristol from Devon, and I drove her north.

On the way through Leominster, we picked Dad up from a funeral home where we'd had him FedExed. He was in a bag, in a box, in a paper bag. He was surprisingly heavy. We squeamishly bought some latex gloves at the Funeral Director's suggestion.

We came into Ludlow, parked at Galedford car park, and met Tim at the train station. Three miles away from Caynham, Ludlow had been our metropolitan centre, our buzzy hub. Ludelaue, it was recorded in 1138, is a 'mound or tumulus by the noisy stream,' from Old English, *hlūde* and *hlāw*. One or two buses a day, so usually the Fiat Panda, clunky tank, Woolworths, Gateways, Kwik Save, the Castle Bookshop, a butcher's with its pheasant braces and rabbit danglings, De Greys teahouse, the Feathers Hotel, squatting like a Jacobean Baba Yaga's hut down on The Bullring, legionella in its waters, royalty in its beds, imperious waiters in the 1980s, threatening those more wealthy than us with crustless cucumber sandwiches. Teenage Mutant Hero Turtle cartoon comics from Doreen Yeo's newsagent on Tower Street. Ludlow Castle, haunted, Market Square, haunted by the smell of cheese and fish. Broad Street, Mill Street, Corve Street, falling into the River Teme, the letters falling off the front of the DIY shop, spelling Ludlow Honecare. Breathless town, humid temporalities, sticky with time, old twelfth-century-and-onwards buildings everywhere, half-timbered, half-day closing, Sandpits housing estate, the town coalescing on a mound above the fields and mud and forests, where the river wound around.

Walking around here, now, a perfect August evening, slightly cold, without him, the new shape of my family felt strange.

We walked past the house where the bees alighted after Mrs Bell's funeral. It dawned on me that we once stayed in that very building, just over ten years after we moved away from Caynham, a February weekend with my brother, his fiancée, my parents, staying in that place with its basement kitchen, making vegetable stews, hot and heavy. We walked along the walls and up the towers of Ludlow Castle in the cold, cold winter wind. We ate at a curry house on Broad Street. I opted for something with so much garlic – 'twelve cloves' it said on the menu – that it gave me indigestion and fiery insomnia.

All weekend I wasn't able to talk because I was so angry and I was angry because I was sad and that had nothing to do with the curry, or the garlic. I slept in the front room of the big house, farting garlic on the pull-out bed, hot and sad with the depression well and truly kicked in. I didn't talk about what was happening. Perhaps I didn't know? Perhaps I couldn't say? By then I probably knew. I had been living in Cornwall, in Falmouth. Depressed, lonely, confused; receiving threatening phone calls late at night from a man – a boy, really, like me – that I had slighted.

Had I? Yes? No? Yes.

That situation was a mess, and so was I. Everyone could tell.

Tim, Mum and I ate dinner in that same curry house on this visit. In the rooms upstairs, Mum told us, there used to be classrooms for evening classes. She took a course taught in those rooms in 1987 or 1988 as part of a scheme where she could both learn and boost our income support from the state.

'Cambridge Certificate in Computer Appreciation,' she said. 'It was a government "retraining for the workplace" scheme, and I got £10 a week. I learned about word processing on Wordstar, spreadsheets on Excel, programming on BBC computers and applications, like how the world was changing as a result of using computers. I did projects on stock control in shops and managing water supplies – water flow from reservoirs in Wales to where it was needed.'

Upstairs the memory of my Mum typing on keyboards, downstairs talking in the restaurant, in the back rooms, tubs of raita, chopped salads, giant pickle jars, diced onions, while further down the street, beyond the old city wall, the River Teme flows wide and fast over the smooth rocks and weir below Ludford Bridge.

On July 27 1739, Sarah Lloyd, urging her pigs into the Teme beneath the bridge for them to wash, slipped on a stone and was swept away. Her husband, Edward, by chance passing by on his way home from work, heard her cries and against advice dived in to save her. 'Neighbours held him by the Arm,' reads the newspaper report, 'yet seeing his wife struggling, he thrust himself out of the Person's Hands, and perished with her... Such an instance of sincere affection as is hardly to be met with,' it concludes. They were buried together in Ludlow the next day.

It brings to mind the aftermath of the accident in the Floating Harbour we had seen from the meeting room at work that November day in Bristol. We found out later that the previous night a woman returning home to their houseboat had fallen into the water, and that her husband had dived in straight after her. He had frozen and drowned looking for her, unaware that she had already managed to climb to safety.

The next morning I drove us 1,749 feet up Titterstone Clee, gaining ground past the last of the quarrymen's cottages and out onto the thin road to the summit, navigating the cattle grids and the sheep, passing the old quarry scars and overgrown railway embankments, the spectre of a car covered in cornflakes.

I parked in a puddle under an exposed rock face. We changed our shoes, and I took the bag from the boot, left the gloves in the back, and locked the car. It was thirty years since we moved to Caynham, twenty-two since we left, and one-hundred-and-sixty-two years, almost to the day, since the Woolhope Club walkers hiked across the same hill on which we now walked.

We made our way past the radars and up to the highest point. We found a spot that somehow felt right. I opened the bag and poured out the contents. And there we sat with Dad; Dad as ashes, Dad as a silent guest, transmuted back to the stuff of the universe, amongst the moss and rocks and lichen and bilberries and roaming sheep.

We chatted idly. It was one of those days on Titterstone, the clear, sunny ones. Bright as fish scales in the sun, only a hint of a haze at the edge of our view. All the landmarks the Woolhopians described were visible, all the field systems and streams, the crannies and the nooks, the gentle rise and fall of the lowlands, all the twinkling windows of the farms and the vague shape of Ludlow, all the August sky and all of the August land. No dog days here, not sultry death of crop, bereft of heat-exhausted birds. A wide, open panorama, little hedgerows and mackerel slippery streams and brooks coursing their wiggly way around us.

Mum picked at the ground – a bit of sheep wool, a bilberry – and dropped it down the little crevice where Dad sat. Votive offerings. I thought about saying goodbye to him in the hospice while I added some grass, a bit of moss.

We sat with Dad for a long time. I got a bit sunburned. It was so peaceful and so strange. It was a bit like being stuck between two frames of film, not wanting the reel to turn and take us on to the rest of the story.

Eventually, though, we had to say our goodbyes and leave, so that Dad could quietly rejoin the world as something new, and so that we could, too.

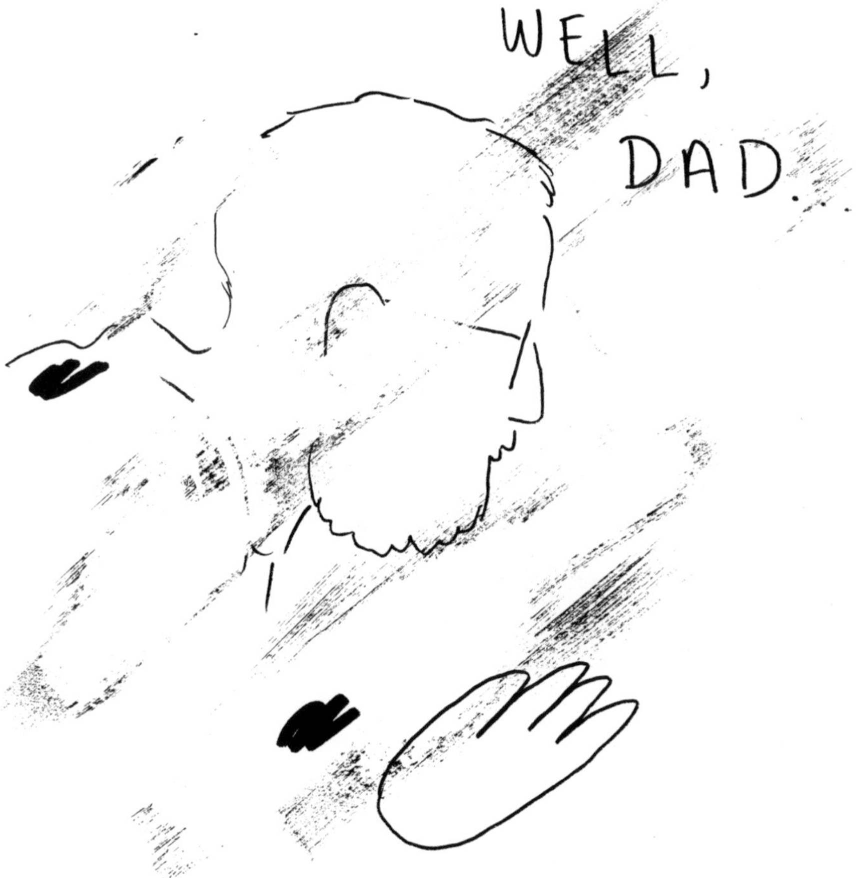
WELL,
DAD...

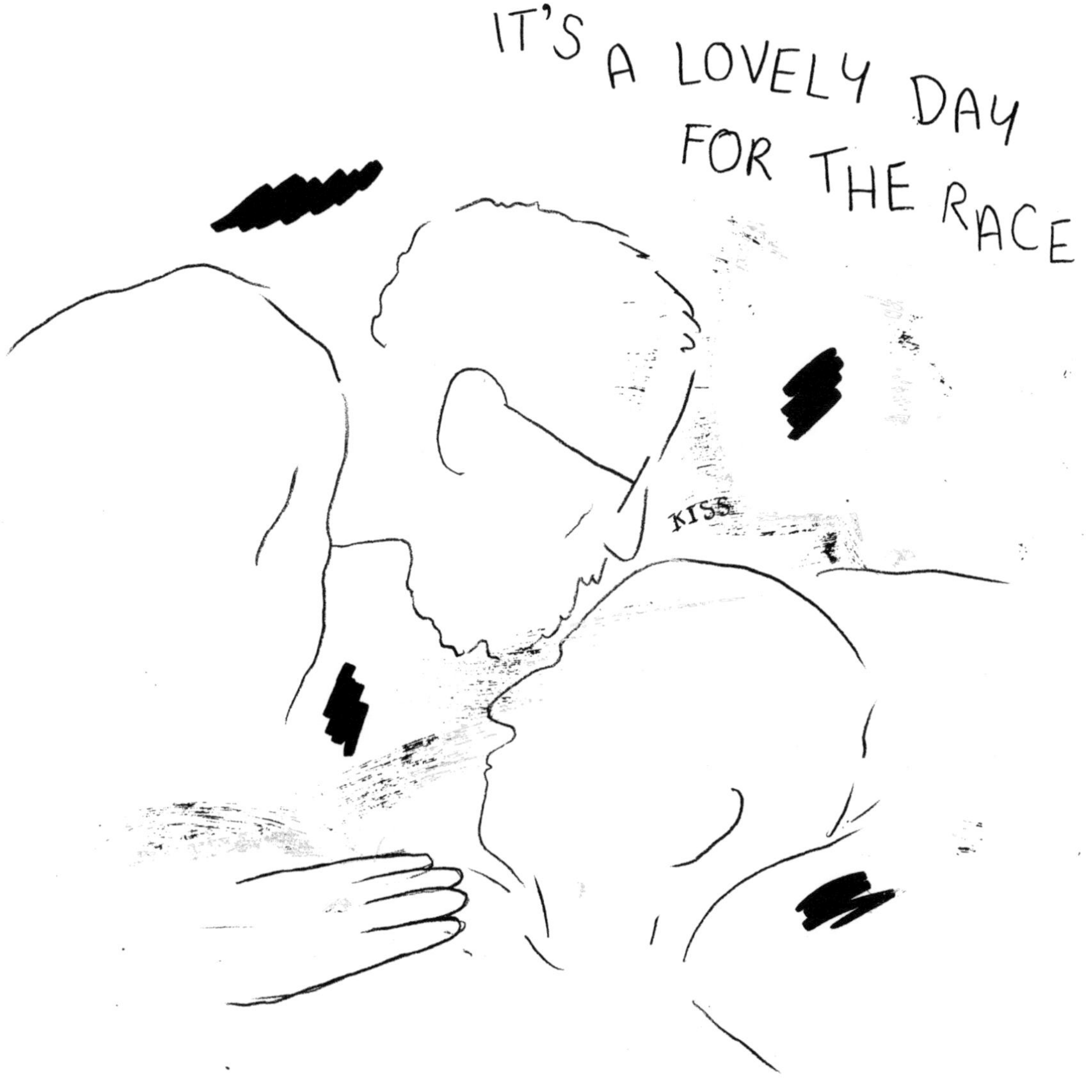
IT'S A LOVELY DAY
FOR THE RACE
KISS

The
End

Epilogue

The year after Dad died, the tomatoes didn't ripen. It had snowed in March and it was cold, late. The earth never warmed up. The seedlings were OK indoors on the windowsill. Then we had a heatwave and I watered them every day. Hottest summer since 1974. Then, the fruit arrived late and stayed green. My friend Nicole said it was because I watered the plants too much, and they spent too much time growing foliage, and not enough time reproducing.

In September I went on a work trip to Tokyo. I thought about Dad as we snaked through the concrete avenues on our way between terminals at Heathrow airport, sat next to my friend Jo on the coach. The ghosts of him and his colleagues were everywhere – echoes of a working life now gone, flickering shades in the long shafts of morning sunlight, in the shadows cast by the overpasses and bridges and catwalks and hangars. We descended into the brutalist jungle of Terminal 4, and I caught sight of a heron, languidly flapping out of the sunrise.

Two weeks later, on my last day in Tokyo, I woke up at 4.30am to a different sunrise. I had a shower, ate some pastries from the 7-Eleven downstairs, got chocolate on my keyboard. A typhoon had come through in the night, making everything sound like being in a car wash. I had woken up at midnight, and looked through the window at the trees outside which were moving like seaweed in a swell, before falling asleep again as the hotel shuddered in sympathy.

I put the memory of the storm to one side. I showered and got dressed, finished packing my suitcase, and double-checked I had all of my belongings. I went down to the lobby to check out and order a taxi. I knew it would be an expensive way to travel, but the public transport was a little scrambled and, honestly, I was, too.

After a short wait, the taxi arrived. I got in, and we pulled out of the hotel. We made our way through the city as the sun came up, the silver buildings reflecting in the water of Tokyo Bay, the shadows of towers in the buttercup-yellow light, the Rainbow Bridge looking as if it was made of marble. As we approached Haneda, I saw planes sleeping in the morning sun and thought about Dad again.

By the time I came back from Japan and the cold had arrived, there was no chance of the tomatoes ripening, not really. There's a family recipe for green tomato chutney, so I asked Mum to send me a photo of it so I could make some. It's written in the blue-covered, blue-lined family recipe book. She sent me images of two versions: the first in Dad's handwriting, annotating a forever shifting recipe, the second a recent revision in my Mum's script – 3lbs of green tomatoes, 5lbs of cooking apples, 3 large onions, 2 1/4lbs of brown sugar, 3 tablespoons of salt, 1 1/4 oz of mustard seed, 3 heaped teaspoons of ground ginger, 3/4lb of sultanas, some chillis, 3 pints of vinegar.

In the months after Dad's death, I made batch after batch of chocolate-chip buns, little sponges like he would make, from his recipe in that same book. Batch after batch. I wanted the smell memory, the taste, remembering the precision with which he baked – never the cook, always the baker. My Mum made the dinners and he made the cakes – I wanted to make something, too, see if I could be as precise as he was.

The same thoughts fill me as I set up shop to make the chutney in the garden, so that the house won't smell of sweaty vinegar onions. I put a big pan on a camping stove, stirring and bubbling the ingredients in the dwindling light. I thought about Dad and me cooking whitebait, him probably the age I am now. I haven't cooked fish in years – I'm vegetarian these days.

Still, he comes to me in surprising ways; I taste my own breath after a cup of Earl Grey tea, a little stale, floral, and it smells like his breath; I do the washing up in the evening and my pride in squaring things away is his memory.

So I've made this book, sneakily writing these words while at work, and I've drawn these pictures, trying to live with the soft pliableness of Dad's memory, and the hyperreal vividness of everything that lead to his death, how scraped into my brain that vividness is, how present all those things still feel.

On Titterstone, the radar station is now largely automated and managed remotely. Every now and then somebody will come to check on it, but mostly the radars just keep themselves to themselves, just like the sheep which still wander around, bleating in the kaleidoscope weather.

Down in Caynham, the woods have been extensively felled and houses – including a six-bedroom mansion – have been built on the remains of the land, a development named 'Caynham Woods'. The redwood now stands on its own in a grassy patch, the woods around it cleared. Houses have also been built on various other territories of our childhood: the wasteland that was the walled garden, the turkey hatchery, everywhere that used to be an open space to traverse from one secret place to another, now all cut into pieces and stitched together with fences and security notices. Apparently, a famous actress now lives in one of the new houses, and in her front garden is the pond that used to sit in the turkey hatchery grounds, overgrown. It's a tasteful landscaping of something that was probably dug for the manor house over two hundred years previously for fish and fowl.

In our old garden, the walnut tree has been cut down. I think it had been looking a bit diseased last time I saw it. Caynham Court is now owned by a vintage firearms dealer and big-game hunting advocate. He and his partner are returning the building and lands to their nineteenth-century state, while the country feels like it's crumbling around us.

He showed me around one day this last September. I saw the old rooms, no longer grainy and dusty, but alive again. I saw the old stairs and the plaster reliefs on the ceiling, and the last of the fake book spines that we'd seen all those years ago, still *in situ* affixed to a door made to look like a bookshelf in what is now the kitchen.

'Dwell on the past and you'll lose an eye,' goes the Russian proverb; 'forget the past and you'll lose both eyes.'

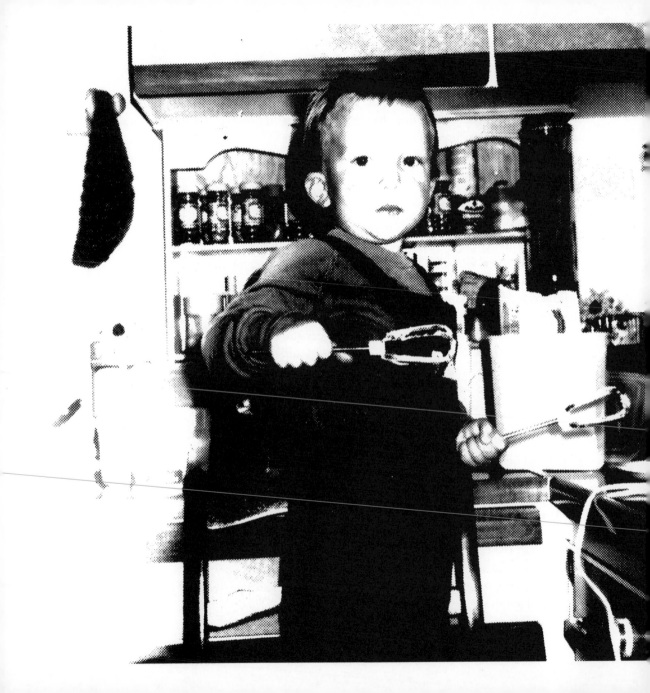

Six weeks after Dad died, Ali and I got married in Bakewell. Our friends Nick and Jo were our witnesses. On our way to the Registration Office, we were in the back seat of Nick and Jo's car. Nick was driving.

As we climbed through the Pennines from Hillsborough, we passed into a forest – cold damp April air and a few green shoots. We came around a bend and a deer, antlers and all, suddenly breached the trees on our right and bounded into the road in front of us.

Nick slowed quickly as the deer gracefully sprang across the carriageway, disappearing into the undergrowth. We cooed and sighed and wooed. I felt humbled and conspicuously human, once more exposed as an animal, despite the pretence of this metal box with wheels.

Ali and I held hands and looked at one another, tears on our cheeks, knowing that for that moment at least, everything was synchronous and significant; everything resonated, and everything was possible.

References

Image Sources

p. 1 Ordnance Survey (1967) Ludlow, sheet 129, 1:25,000. Chessington: Ordnance Survey.

p. 2 Baker, O. (1906) *Ludlow: Town and Neighbourhood* Ludlow: G. Woolley (p. 122).

pp. 32–33 Tithe map of Cainham [Caynham] (parish), Shropshire. National Archives Ref: IR 30/29/63.

pp. 34–35 Titterstone and Caynham Camp, 30/01/1966. Cambridge University Aerial Photograph Archive: www.cambridgeairphotos.com.

pp. 36, 37, 60 Moreton, T. (1991) *My House Ludlow*: self-published (pp. 1, 2, 5).

p. 77 Arnold, N. Ovenden, D. and Corbet, G. (1986) *A Handguide to the Wild Animals of Britain Europe* London: Treasure Press (p. 110).

p. 77 Harris, J. (1990) *Pocket Guide to Wildlife of Britain and Europe* London: Kingfisher Books (p. 8).

p. 83–85 Stephenson, T. ed (1941) *The Countryside Companion* London: Odhams Press (pp. 94, 95, 96).

p. 93 Chambers, E. K. (1903) *The Mediaeval Stage* Oxford: The Clarendon Press (p. 116).

p. 94 Blanche, D. (1922) *Star of Mercia; historical tales of Wales and the marches* London: Jonathan Cape (p. 131).

pp. 100, 109 Burne, C. S. (1886) *Shropshire Folk-lore; A Sheaf of Gleanings Vol 3* Shrewsbury: Trübner and Co. (p. 376).

p. 128 *Birmingham Daily Gazette* (1955) 'This is the sort of lad we want' Industry Welcomes Products of F. B. C. Training Scheme. *Birmingham Daily Gazette*, Wednesday, 20 July.

pp. 155, 195 Jenkins, A (1983) *Titterstone Clee Hills: Everyday Life, Industrial History and Dialect* Orleton: Alf Jenkins Publications (p. 8).

p. 168 manipulated version of Herring Sr., J. F. (1839) *Fox Hunting: Encouraging Hounds* [oil on panel] Yale Center for British Art, Paul Mellon Collection.

pp. 209–214 Shropshire farmer Buck Allport talks to John Swallow on ATV Today in 1976 https://player.bfi.org.uk/free/film/watch-buck-allport-1976-online.

pp. 222–223 *Caynham Court: Seat of Captain Berkeley Calcott*, engraved by T. Radcliffe after F. Page *c.* 1850.

pp. 224–226 Leach, F. (1891) *The County Seats Of Shropshire* Shrewsbury: Eddowe's Shrewsbury Journal (pp. 93–94).

p. 232 The library at Caynham Court, 1870 (Historic England Archives) Item ref: 5048/7.

p.244 Handford, B. (1986) *Lancing College History and Memoirs* Chichester: Phillimore and Co (p. 238).

p. 248 Barraclough, P. (1927) *James Herbert Croft* [Oil on Canvas] Hereford, UK: Croft Castle.

p. 249 Western Morning News (1941) 'Baronet Found Shot' *Western Morning News*, Monday 18 August.

p. 266 Country Life (1977) Sale notice for Nash Court, *Country Life Supplement*, March 3 (p. 27).

p. 275 Podmore, F. (1897) *Studies in Psychical Research* London: G. P. Putnam's Sons (pp. 254).

p. 305 Fortean Times (1994) 'Bees Pay Last Respects' *Fortean Times* 78, December (p. 10).

p. 311 Hartshorne, C. H. (1841) *Salopia antiqua: or, An enquiry from personal survey into the 'druidical', military, and other early remains in Shropshire and the north Welsh borders*. London: J. W. Parker (p. 25).

p. 312 Public Ledger and Daily Advertiser (1826) 'Court of King's Bench, November 1: libel the John Bull newspaper' *Public Ledger and Daily Advertiser* Monday 20 November.

p. 320 Tourist guide to Ludlow (undated).

Further Reading

Baker, O. (1906) *Ludlow: Town and Neighbourhood* Ludlow: G. Woolley.

Bennett, G. (2001) Charlotte Sophia Burne: Shropshire Folklorist, First Woman President of the Folklore Society, and First Woman Editor of Folklore. Part 2: Update and Preliminary Bibliography. *Folklore* 112, 95–106. www.doi.org.

Burke, J. (1836) A *Genealogical and Heraldic History of the Commoners of Great Britain and Ireland Enjoying Territorial Possessions Or High Official Rank: But Uninvested with Heritable Honours.* London: Colburn.

Denison, S. (2005) *Quarry Land: Impermanent Landscapes of the Clee Hills,* Greyscale Books.

Forrest, H. E. (1924) *Some old Shropshire houses and their owners: a series of papers reprinted from the Transactions of the Shropshire archæological society and of the Caradoc field club (with 45 illustrations).*

Forrest, H. E. (1899) *The fauna of Shropshire, being an account of all the mammals, birds, reptiles & fishes found in the county of Salop.* Shrewsbury: L. Wilding.

Burne, C. S. (ed), (1883) *Shropshire Folk-lore: A Sheaf of Gleanings* (Vol 1–3). Shrewsbury: Trübner & co.

Goodman, K. G. W. (1978) *Hammerman's Hill: the Land, People and Industry of Titterstone Clee Hill Area of Shropshire from the Sixteenth to the Eighteenth Centuries.* PhD thesis Keele: University of Keele.

Hartshorne, C. H. (1841) *Salopia antiqua: or, An enquiry from personal survey into the 'druidical,' military, and other early remains in Shropshire and the north Welsh borders.* London: J. W. Parker.

Hayward, L. H. (1938) Shropshire Folklore of Yesterday and To-Day. *Folklore* 49, 223–243.

Jackson, G. F. (1879) *Shropshire word-book, a glossary of archaic and provincial words, etc., used in the county.* Shrewsbury: Trübner & co.

Jenkins, A. (1983) *Titterstone Clee Hills: Everyday Life, Industrial History and Dialect* Orleton: Alf Jenkins Publications.

Leland, J., in Smith, L. T. (1907) *The itinerary of John Leland in or about the years 1535–1543.* Edited by Lucy Toulmin Smith. London: G. Bell.

Swainson, C. (1886) *The folklore and provincial names of British birds.* London, Pub. for the Folk-lore Society by E. Stock.

Timmins, H. T. (1899) *Nooks and corners of Shropshire.* London: Elliot Stock.

Wright, T. (1854) *Wanderings of an antiquary; chiefly upon the traces of the Romans in Britain.* London: J. B. Nichols.

Wright, T. (1826) *The History & Antiquities of the Town of Ludlow, and Its Ancient Castle: with Lives of the Presidents, and Descriptive and Historical Accounts of Gentlemen's Seats, Villages, &c:* Procter and Jones.

Acknowledgements

This book was initially published in four hand-made instalments as part of my ongoing zine series, *Minor Leagues*. I'd print copies out on my creaking laser printer, wolfing through toner, hand-folding French flaps into card covers and stapling sheafs together to make big chunky one-hundred-page book things. I'd send them across the world to an extremely modest but supportive readership, and swap tales over emails and letters about the stories I was telling. Making stuff myself in this way is my first love. But sometimes you make something and hope more people will want to see it than you can reach on your own. So my first thanks for taking on this task go to Gracie, Graham, Adrian and Jon at Little Toller Books, who are wonderful. I'm also indebted to Max Porter, without whose quiet behind-the-scenes championing I would not have met Little Toller, nor found the confidence in the book I eventually discovered.

The book itself only took this form and went down the rabbit holes it did because of my friend Meriel, whose serendipitous appearance in Bristol many years after we first met brought with it connections, Charlotte Sophia Burne, the Woolhopians, and so much more. Hats off to Maxim Peter Griffin for the inspiration (onwards); to 'Woofferton Steve' whom I met at the Wicked Grin in Ludlow for the fact-checking;

Diggory Hadoke for showing me around refurbished Caynham Court thirty years after my brother and I first got dusty in its old colonial shell; Phil Murden for telling me about my Dad; to Anna Howorth for coincidences; to Tom for the translation of the Latin inscription found on Maria Powell's tomb; to the subscribers and readers of *Minor Leagues* and to Warren and the Weird Comics gang for keeping me going; to Andy Oliver, Mike Fournier, Tom Murphy, and everyone else who wrote nice things about the book before it became a book, and to you all for reading this thing. Finally, thanks to Hospiscare and all the staff at the Royal Devon and Exeter Hospital who took care of my Dad so boldly and warmly during his illness and at the end.

All my love forever to my Mum and my brother and to my family, to Ali for absolutely everything, and to my Dad for being who he was – and Dad, please don't worry; I've found myself – I'm hidden in Surrey.

S. M.
Bristol, 2021

THROUGH THE WOODS *H. E. Bates*
MEN AND THE FIELDS *Adrian Bell*
HAVERGEY *John Burnside*
ORISON FOR A CURLEW *Horatio Clare*
SOMETHING OF HIS ART: WALKING WITH J. S. BACH *Horatio Clare*
ARBOREAL: WOODLAND WORDS *Adrian Cooper*
ISLAND YEARS, ISLAND FARM *Frank Fraser Darling*
LANDFILL *Tim Dee*
HERBACEOUS *Paul Evans*
THE TREE *John Fowles*
TIME AND PLACE *Alexandra Harris*
THE MAKING OF THE ENGLISH LANDSCAPE *W. G. Hoskins*
FARMER'S YEAR *Clare Leighton*
FOUR HEDGES *Clare Leighton*
DREAM ISLAND *R. M. Lockley*
EMPERORS, ADMIRALS AND CHIMNEY SWEEPERS *Peter Marren*
THE UNOFFICIAL COUNTRYSIDE *Richard Mabey*
RING OF BRIGHT WATER *Gavin Maxwell*
DIARY OF A YOUNG NATURALIST *Dara McAnulty*
WHERE? *Simon Moreton*
A SEA STORY *Louisa Adjoa Parker*
LOVE, MADNESS, FISHING *Dexter Petley*
THE LONG FIELD *Pamela Petro*
THE ASH TREE *Oliver Rackham*
ANCIENT WOODS OF THE HELFORD RIVER *Oliver Rackham*
LIMESTONE COUNTRY *Fiona Sampson*
MY HOUSE OF SKY: THE LIFE OF J. A. BAKER *Hetty Saunders*
SNOW *Marcus Sedgwick*
WATER AND SKY, RIDGE AND FURROW *Neil Sentance*
BLACK APPLES OF GOWER *Iain Sinclair*
BEYOND THE FELL WALL *Richard Skelton*
CORNERSTONES: SUBTERRANEAN WRITING *Mark Smalley*
FARMER'S GLORY *A. G. Street*
IN PURSUIT OF SPRING *Edward Thomas*
ON SILBURY HILL *Adam Thorpe*
THE NATURAL HISTORY OF SELBORNE *Gilbert White*
NO MATTER HOWMANY SKIES HAVE FALLEN *Ken Worpole*
GHOST TOWN: A LIVERPOOL SHADOWPLAY *Jeff Young*

Little Toller Books

FORD, PINEAPPLE LANE, DORSET
w. littletoller.co.uk   e. books@littletoller.co.uk